Collage

a Step by Step Guide

Valerie Janitch

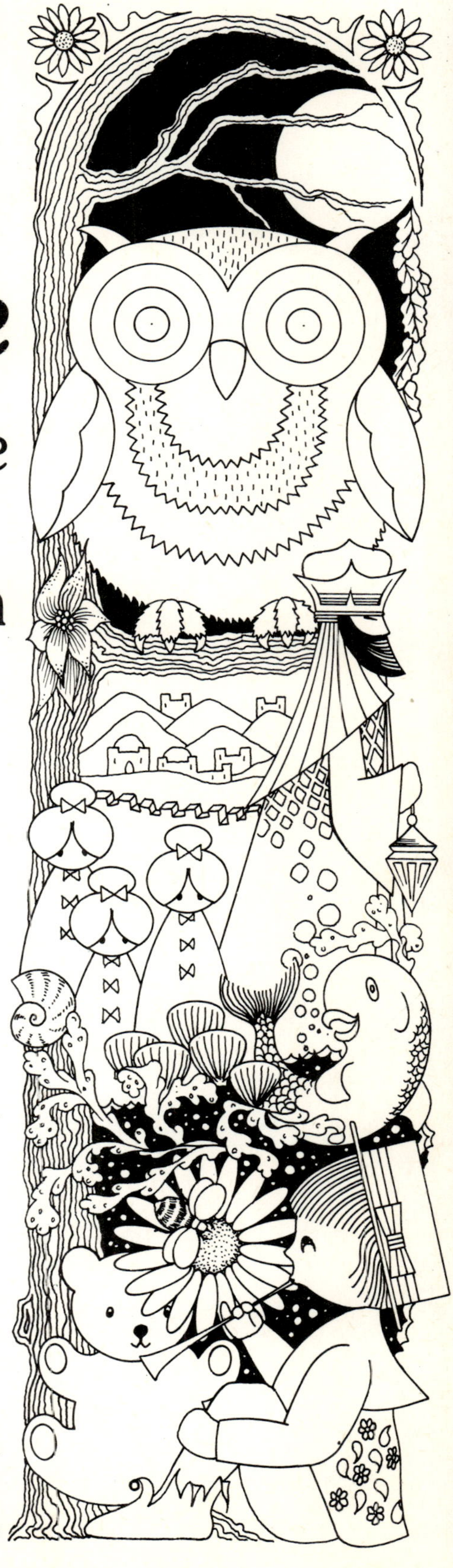

HAMLYN

London · New York · Sydney · Toronto

Contents

Published by
The Hamlyn Publishing Group Ltd.
London · New York · Sydney · Toronto
Astronaut House, Feltham, Middlesex, England.

Second impression 1975
ISBN 0 600 38097 1
Printed in England by
Chapel River Press, Andover, Hampshire

1 What is collage? 4
Why you don't have to be an artist to do collage: why your collages can't help being truly individual: how simple beginnings develop: dainty and romantic – or bold and strong?: how to use this book: the equipment you will need: adhesives: backgrounds: framing: tracing and transferring tracings

2 Begin in the nursery 7
Mr. Woo – the Colourful Owl
'Mary, Mary, Quite Contrary . . .'

3 Developing the detail 16
Red Indians at Home
Edwardiana

4 Composing a picture 30
The Houses on the Hill
Bedtime Story

5 Drawing from nature 38
Summer Garden
Flowers in the Sun

6 Flights of fancy 42
Pair of Turtle Doves
Bird of Paradise

7 Sophisticated simplicity 48
Snowscape
Daisies

8 Assemblage 55
Reading Matter
Country Memories

9 Unusual techniques 59
The Ocean Bed
'Stained Glass' Tudor Rose

10 Unmounted wallhangings 66
Weather House
Tudor Lady

11 Practical applications 72
Aquarium Lampshade
Christmas and general occasion greetings cards
'Ivy Trails' place mats

12 Grande finale 76
'Love Story'

Introduction

There's so little to say about collage . . . and so much to do! Once you know the basic method, and have gathered together the few necessary items of equipment, you can start to experiment. And then you will begin to appreciate the endless scope and freedom you have in your choice of materials – and discover the various techniques of the craft for yourself.

This book guides you from your first simple steps in collage to really ambitious projects which you might have thought were beyond your ability. But that's the secret of collage: it *grows*. And almost before you realise it, you find your work developing to create spectacular results. But the beauty of collage can also lie in its simplicity, and right from the beginning you will be composing charming pictures which will give you splendid creative satisfaction, as well as delighting your family and friends.

1 What is collage?

The word comes from the French *coller*: to paste or glue – and it is simply the technique of creating a picture, design or decoration by sticking or otherwise attaching *anything at all* which contributes to building up the complete arrangement. Collage covers such a wide range of exciting possibilities, and there are so few rules, that it is impossible to be more specific than that.

Why you don't have to be an artist to do collage Instead of sitting down with a blank canvas in front of you and only a brush in your hand, you are able to use the design of fabrics, lace, braid, jewelery and so on to create your picture. This book helps you to begin – by giving you patterns for your basic designs, with working instructions for each one.

Why your collages can't help being truly individual The majority of the materials and trimmings you use will come from your own collection of bits and pieces (enthusiastic collagers are inveterate hoarders!). This is the beauty of collage – and the thing that makes it so satisfying. So **your** collage won't be exactly like mine: it can't be. . . . But instead, it will be just as personal to you, and the materials will evoke just as many happy or amusing memories, as mine for me.

How simple beginnings develop Having started off with the basic patterns in the book, you will soon find your own collage developing in a – sometimes startlingly – different way to the finished version in the illustration. Although this is initially due to the fact that you are using your own materials, you will also find that once you have your basic design to build on, you will immediately begin to visualise the scope for further development and decoration. Which may lead in a completely different direction to the one I have taken. It is the flexibility and freedom of collage that makes *your* work always original and individual.

Dainty and romantic – or bold and strong? If you study the work of other people (as you are sure to do as your interest grows), you will soon notice the difference in styles. Some artists enjoy working with delicate fabrics, lace and tiny trimmings, whilst others prefer nuts and bolts and cog-wheels! My own preference is for the daintier effects and romantic subjects – but you will find that as you gain experience in the general technique of collage, you are developing your own style, and your treatment will more and more reflect your own personality.

How to use this book

If you are completely new to collage – begin at the beginning. Each design is given in pattern form – in most cases to be traced – and there are step-by-step working instructions, accompanied by diagrams illustrating each stage in the development. Starting with the first very simple picture, you will progress as each succeeding chapter introduces a new technique or treatment. So that by the end of the book you will have a thorough working knowledge of the various aspects of the craft. Of course, it isn't necessary to **do** every collage – but as each one contributes something new, you will find it worth reading the text and studying the diagrams, so that you don't miss anything you might need to know later.

The equipment you will need

You will want tracing paper (see below), medium-weight Vilene or Pellon, a fairly small pair of really accurate, sharp scissors, with a larger pair for cutting out heavier materials, tweezers, pins, pencils (soft and hard), eraser, measure, etcetera – and the appropriate brushes and spreaders for your adhesives (see below).

Adhesives

These are most important, and it is essential to use the right one for the job if you want a professional finish. It is the development of modern adhesives which has largely contributed to the joys of collage, making it much easier than in the days of messy brown glues. I use a do-it-yourself fabric adhesive for much of my work, with an all-purpose clear adhesive for non-porous and some other items. Wallpaper paste is invaluable – and has the added advantage of never leaving a stain, no matter how much paste you get in the wrong places. Occasionally I find double-sided tape useful for applying very fine items, like feathers or dried grass heads or lace – and a strong tape helps to join sections together neatly.

Backgrounds

A word about the base on which your collage is mounted may be helpful at this stage – although I have described **my** own bases and background coverings for each specific design in the instructions.

The base must be firm and flat, and of course the most obvious choice is a piece of stiff card, hardboard or wood: but I find good card very expensive, especially as one needs really heavy board to prevent curling. Wood too, is expensive if you haven't a suitable piece and need to buy it – and **I'll** do anything to avoid using it anyway, as I'm incapable of sawing a straight line!

My solution to these problems – which I appreciate may not be yours – may seem odd, but I find it extremely satisfactory. I use cake stands. The ordinary papier mâché, silver-covered boards which are sold for birthday, wedding or any other kind of party cake. They are firm and flat, thick (usually about $\frac{1}{2}$ inch), the composition inside is soft enough to drive pins into (this is a great advantage), and they can be bought in various sizes, either circular or square. They also form an ideal basis for framing and hanging, needing no additional backing. For rectangular pictures, I simply cut a square stand to shape. And cost-wise, they are little more expensive than heavy card or wood.

To cover your mount with background fabric (or paper), place the board on it and cut the fabric 1–2 inches larger all round (see individual examples). Remove the board and press the fabric.

If you are following my example and using silver-covered cake stands, place your fabric over the stand to check whether you can see a slight "sparkle" from the silver paper underneath. If so, paste a piece of paper – preferably the same colour as your fabric – over the stand: I use coloured tissue, but any paper will do.

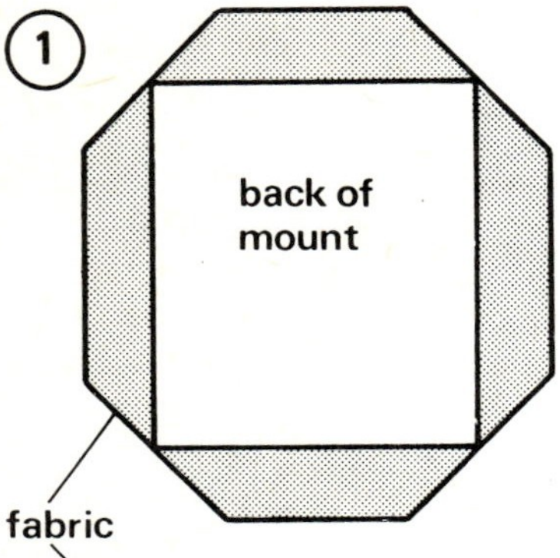

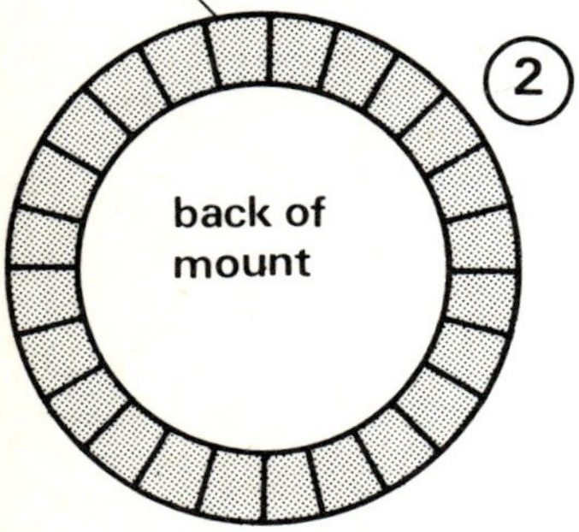

Now coat the surface of your board thoroughly with wallpaper and then place the fabric centrally on top, smoothing out any wri Turn the board over and take the surplus fabric over the sides round to the back as follows.

For straight-sided, square or rectangular mounts, mitre the corne (cut away a triangle across each corner as diagram 1), then draw the fabric neatly over and stick to the back with fabric adhesive.

For circular or curved mounts, snip the surplus fabric into small tabs all the way round (as diagram 2), then draw each separate tab neatly over and stick to the back with fabric adhesive.

If you are using felt as a background fabric, and are trimming the edge with braid, you may prefer to cut the felt the same size as your mount, so that the edge of the felt is level with the edges of the mount – and to stick it down with fabric adhesive.

Framing

Unless you have an endless supply of friends and relatives – and remember all their birthdays – once you become addicted to collage, the walls of your home will gradually begin to resemble those of an art gallery! So it is necessary to be strict with oneself, and limit your exhibition at any one time to a tasteful selection of one's work. However, if you have gone to the expense of having your work professionally glazed and framed, you will understandably feel that they are of more lasting value. To avoid this predicament, I deliberately regard the majority of my work as having only a limited life – so that I can keep replacing collages I have become accustomed to with new ones (you can either store the old ones to reappear again in the future, or give them away – you'll find no shortage of eager recipients!). So throughout this book you will find that the instructions describe how to complete the picture with a braid or other form of "frame" or finished edge, avoiding any additional expense. Fix rings or tabs at the back to hang.

Of course, if you want to protect your collage with glass, and frame it properly, just ignore my finishing instructions.

Tracing – and transferring tracings

Before you begin, there is just one essential thing you need to know. You probably had to trace so many maps in school that the remainder of this paragraph is superfluous – but as it is very important to make absolutely accurate tracings, here is the method I use.

Tracing paper can be bought from stationers – or you can use ordinary household greaseproof paper or good quality white tissue paper.

Fix the paper over the pattern you want to trace so that it won't slip, and draw over the required outlines with a sharp pencil.

Remove the tracing, and if you want to transfer it, rub over the lines on the *back* of the paper with a soft lead pencil. Then place it, right side up, flat on the paper or other material on which you want to reproduce it – and draw over the lines again with a hard pencil. When you lift the tracing, an impression of the shape you have marked should remain.

Incidentally, if the design happens to be identical on both the left and right of the pattern (see Mr. Woo – page 8), it will be reversible. In this case you can save yourself trouble by simply turning your original tracing over and drawing over the *back* with a hard pencil to transfer it: but be careful not to do this unless you actually **want** to reverse a design – to make a figure face in the opposite direction, for instance.

When working in fabric, you will need to trace *patterns*: I find good quality white tissue paper is best for this.

2 Begin in the nursery

To introduce you to the basic method of collage, I have designed two pictures with the nursery in mind – though they would look gay anywhere in the home: the owl in the kitchen, perhaps, and the nursery rhyme in a pretty bedroom.

The first collage is a very easy one in paper – the second takes you on to fabric. I have described the method of working each one in the greatest detail, so that each stage will be absolutely clear. Your own common sense will make a lot of this obvious, but I want to clarify each point at every stage in this first chapter, because it provides the basis for the rest of the book.

Mr. Woo-the Colourful Owl

Illustrated in colour on page 17

For your very first collage, I have designed an amusing owl made up entirely of gaily contrasting papers. Packets of assorted coloured papers are sold for children, and unless you happen to have a range of coloured papers already, this is much cheaper than buying whole sheets of cartridge paper from art shops: this is only sensible for large areas of background, or if you want a particular colour. Mr. Woo comes very happily out of such a packet – which gives you such a wide choice that you may well decide on a completely different colour scheme from the one I have chosen. If you do, then you will already be discovering the flexibility of collage – and the way in which you will want to adapt all the basic designs in this book to suit your own personality.

Although Mr. Woo is very simple and straightforward – the method is exactly the same as for any collage. So I have illustrated the working order with step-by-step diagrams, so that once you have followed these, you will understand the basic directions for all the designs to come – which are only developments and variations on the same basic technique.

Materials: Coloured papers in donkey brown, violet, cyclamen, pale pink, dark blue, light blue, orange, deep yellow, light yellow, two or three shades of green, and black
8 in. diameter round cake stand – or circle of stiff card
8 in. diameter circular wooden bag handle for frame (optional) – or $\frac{3}{4}$ yd. contrasting braid
Wallpaper paste
Clear all-purpose adhesive

Method: Cut a piece of tracing paper a little larger than the master pattern of the owl (diagram 1).

Trace the *outline* shape only (A – diagram 2). Then transfer to brown paper and cut out (as this design is identical on both left and right, remember that in this case you can keep reversing your tracing instead of marking the back with a soft pencil).

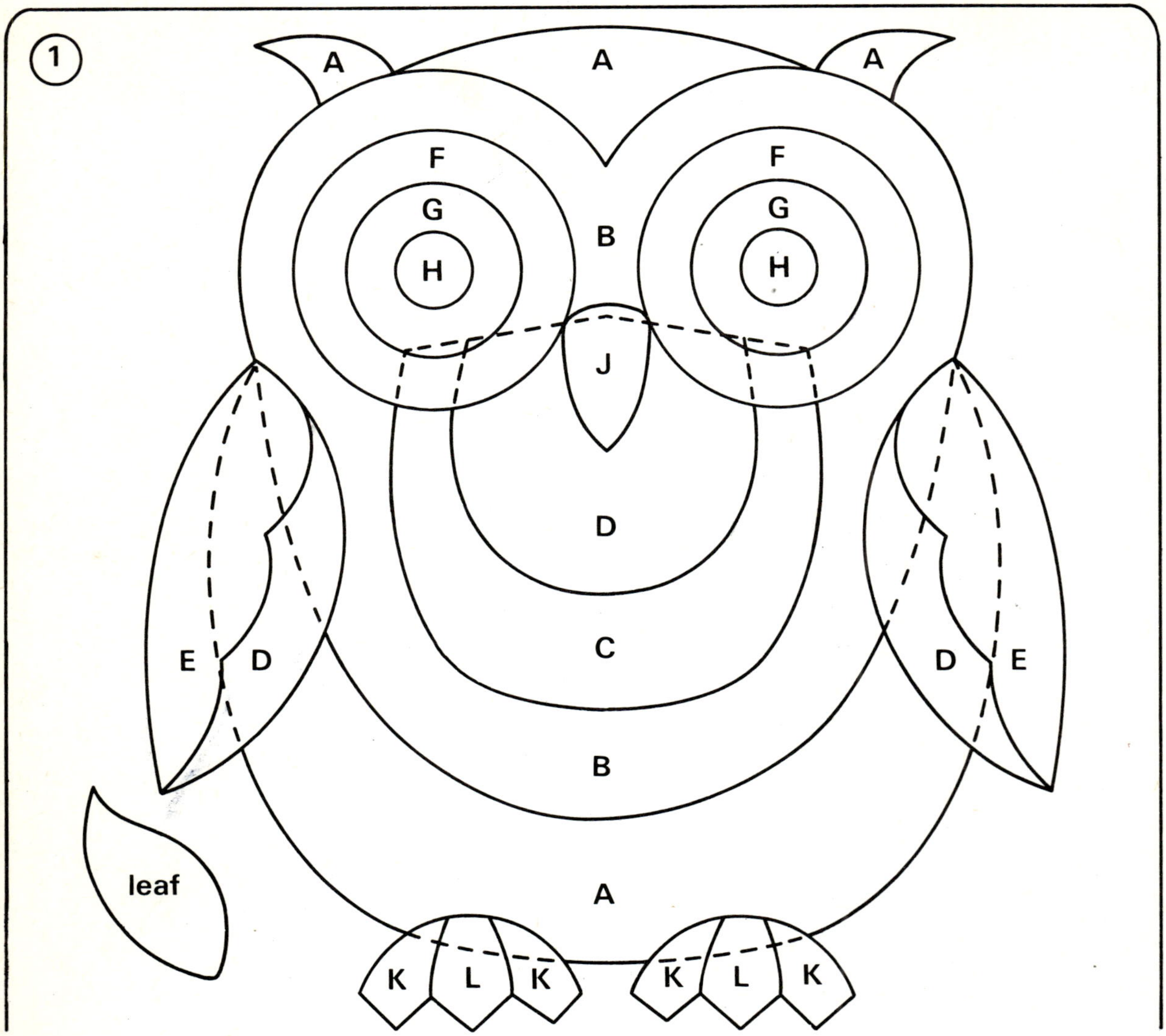

Now take your tracing back to the master pattern, carefully re-align it over the outline shape, and trace the whole of section B – following the broken lines under the wings (diagram 3). Using your tracing, mark the position of this piece faintly on your brown shape (diagram 4). Then use the tracing again to transfer the shape to a piece of violet paper, and cut it out. (Incidentally, I used pinking shears to cut the lower edges of the chest pieces, to add interest). Paste the violet shape carefully into position, following the pencil indication (diagram 5). Trim any overlapping edges neatly.

Return to the master pattern again, re-align your tracing, and trace the middle section of the chest (C) – following the broken lines at each side and across the top (diagram 6). Mark the position on the previous violet section as before, then cut in cyclamen and paste into position (diagram 7).

In the same way, trace and mark the top chest piece and the *whole* wing at each side (sections D – diagram 8). Cut these three pieces in pale pink and paste into position following exactly the same procedure (diagram 9).

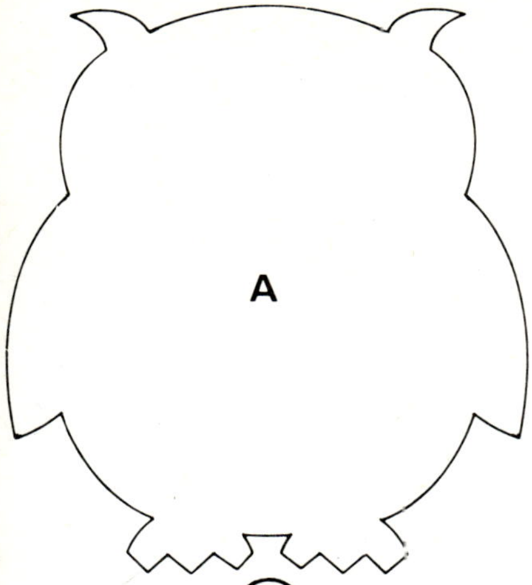

2

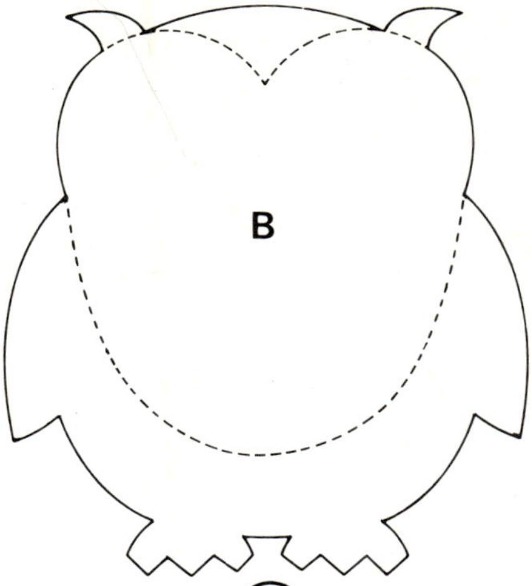

3

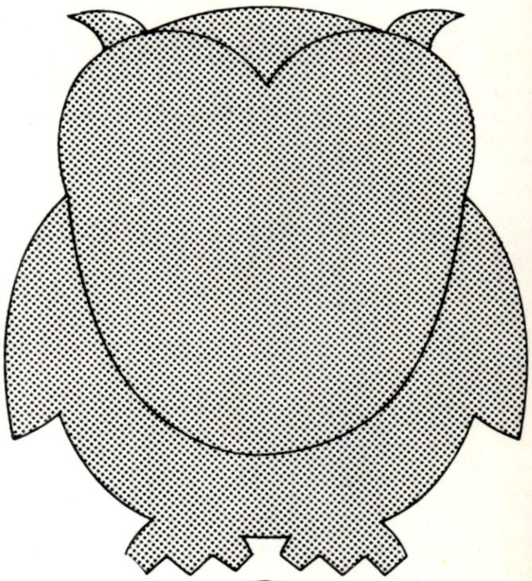

4

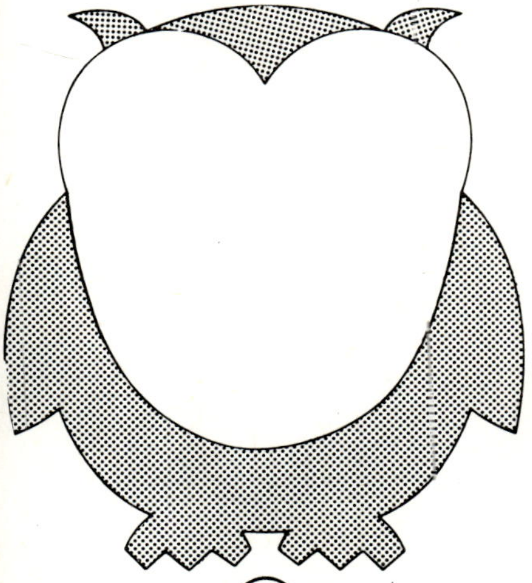

5

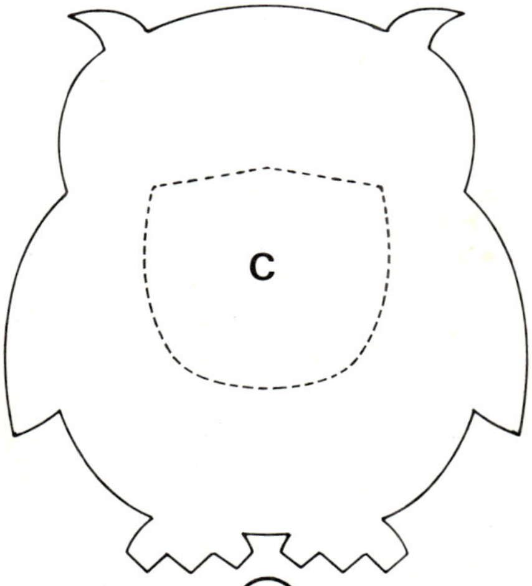

6

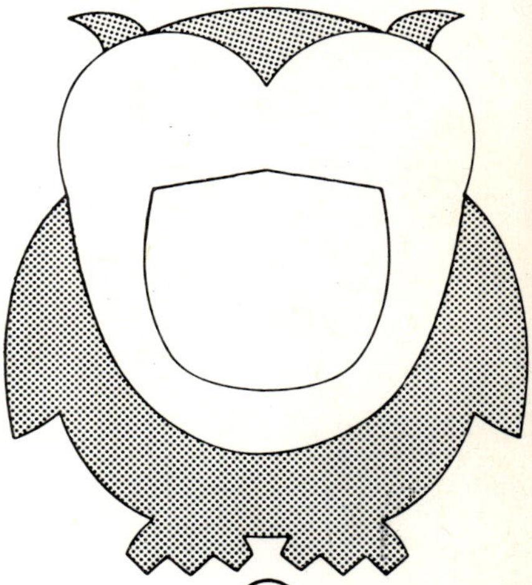

7

Trace and cut the outer section of each wing in brown (sections E – diagram 10), and paste over the pink at each side, level with the cut edge (diagram 11).

Cut two circles in dark blue for the outer eyes (F – diagram 10): mark positions and paste down (diagram 11).

Cut smaller circles in pale blue for the inner eyes (G – diagram 12): mark position on the outer eyes and paste down, followed by tiny black circles (H – diagram 12) for the pupils (diagram 13).

Trace and mark the beak (J): cut in orange, and paste into place (diagram 13).

Cut the *whole* of each foot (K – diagram 12) in deep yellow. Paste down, then add the centre section only (L) in light yellow (diagram 13).

Outline the beak and mark the feet into sections with a black felt pen, if necessary for clearer definition.

Cover an 8 in. diameter cake stand (or circle of card) with black paper, allowing $\frac{1}{2}$ in. to overlap all round the edge. Cut this surplus into tabs all the way round, and stick to the sides or back.

Mount the completed owl carefully down on the circle, the feet about

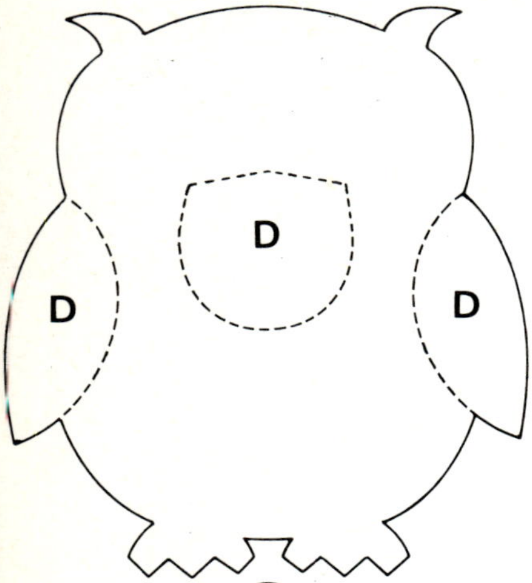

8

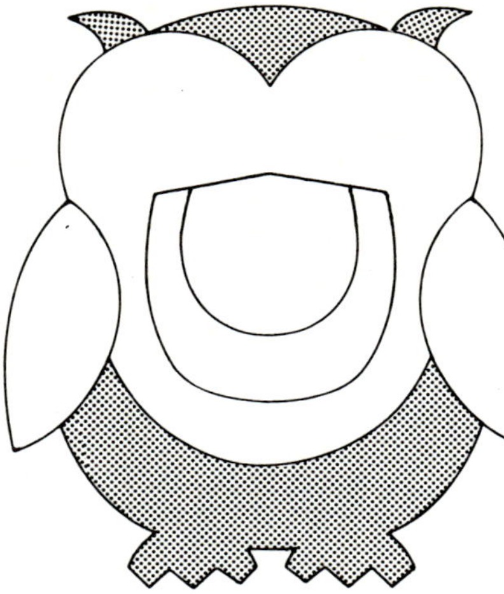

9

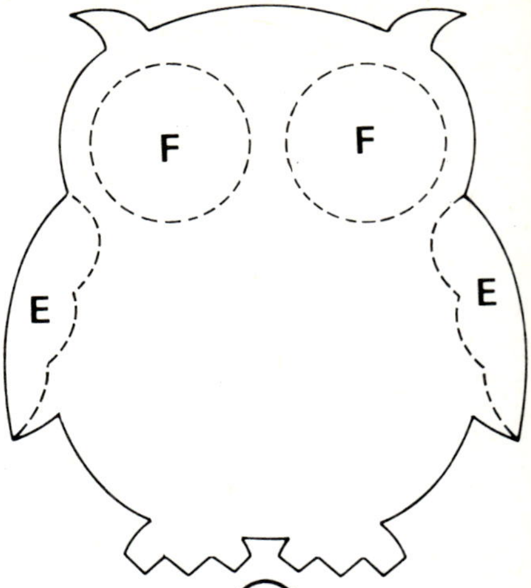

10

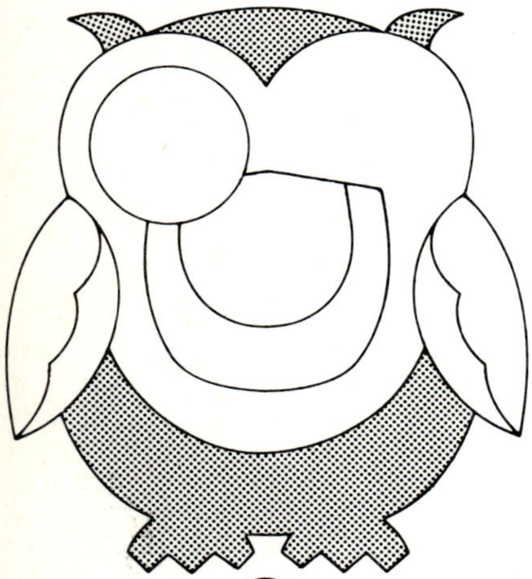

11

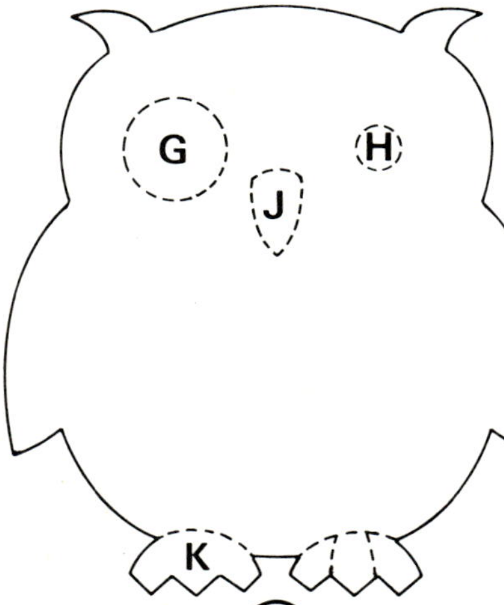

12

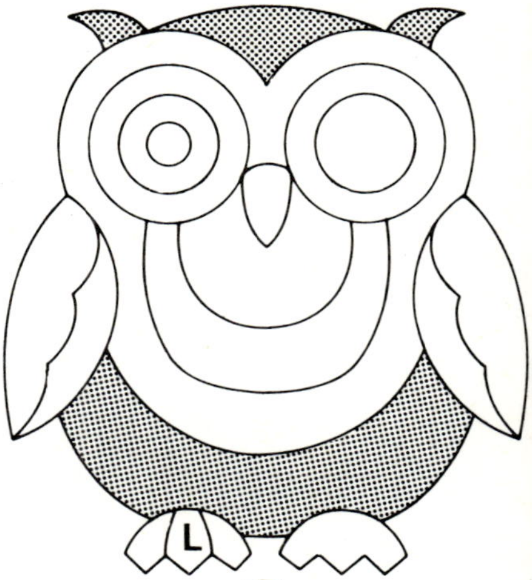

13

1 inch from the edge.

Trace the leaf and cut about sixteen times in two or three shades of green, reversing the pattern to cut alternate shapes. Stick in groups round the owl, as illustrated.

Using an all-purpose clear adhesive, stick the wooden handle – or braid – round the edge of the circle to form a frame.

Working with fabric

Now for your first picture in fabric. This is probably the most popular form of collage – and certainly one of the most enjoyable to do. It is particularly suitable for human figures – since the clothes are actually made of fabric – and it offers endless scope for imaginative use of trimmings, sequins, bits of old costume jewelery and similar odds and ends. You can usually find the fabrics you want in your own piece bag – and once friends know you are enthusiastic, you will find yourself inundated with **their** dress cuttings and broken jewelery, too. In fact, the only disadvantage is that, the keener you become, the more your hoarding instincts develop: you can't bear to throw **anything** away!

'Mary, Mary, Quite Contrary...'

Illustrated in colour on page 17

Here is a simple – yes, it really is simple – design worked mainly in felt, which is lovely to use because it doesn't fray – and is thick enough to prevent the adhesive soaking through if you use too much. I have trimmed the figures with bits of broderie Anglaise, lace, braid and so on, from my own collection. Your trimmings will obviously differ – but that is the beauty of collage, and the thing that makes it so personal. So if, for instance, you haven't any suitable bits of broderie Anglaise for the pantaloons, use wide lace or two or three overlapping rows of very narrow lace – or white fabric, adding a band of narrow lace along the lower edge. Similarly, she could be wearing a plain dress with a patterned pinafore and her bonnet could be trimmed round the back, instead of the front of the brim. And of course, your colour scheme is sure to be quite different: just make sure the figures will stand out well against your background colour.

The figures are made up individually – like the owl – on a Vilene or Pellon backing, only being mounted down when they are complete. This means you avoid making mistakes which can't be rectified (if the worst happens, you can always start again), and you won't risk ruining the background with a blob of adhesive or a grubby mark. It allows much sharper edges, too – and you can take the cut ends of trimmings neatly round to the back. You will be doing this in later designs, but note the advantage when you add the braid tie to the front of the boy's tunic in this one. If you haven't any Vilene or Pellon, substitute white cartridge paper: but do *try* to use Vilene or Pellon because it is so much softer and more flexible, making it easier to work with.

You will notice that I use pink face tissue for flesh areas: this is purely a personal preference, and thicker paper, fabric or felt would all do as well. But I find the tissue gives a pleasantly delicate texture – and allows one to add features in ink, which one cannot do on fabric or felt, which must be embroidered.

Incidentally, this design was inspired by a packet of tiny coloured shells which took my eye in the aquaria section of a pet shop. If you haven't any suitable small shells, you could always cut shell shapes from large sequins or stiff pastel-coloured paper.

Unless otherwise specified, use a do-it-yourself fabric adhesive throughout.

Materials:

- Medium-weight Vilene or Pellon
- Felt in deep yellow, dark blue, mid-blue, browns, grey, black and white
- Brown fabric or felt for boy's hair
- Fabric for girl's dress
- Broderie Anglaise, lace or white fabric for girl's pinafore and pantaloons
- Lace, braid, flowers, as required, to trim bonnet
- Lace or fabric for "pretty maids"
- Braids to trim boy's suit
- Natural raffia or straw for boater
- Pink twin-ply face tissue
- Tiny coloured shells (or mother-of-pearl sequins, pastel-coloured papers, etcetera)
- Silver sequins or studs about $\frac{3}{8}$ in. diameter

Materials: (cont.)	Tiny seed pearls Lace and/or tiny artificial flowers 12 in. square cake stand – or a piece of stiff card 12 ins. by 9 ins. Felt or fabric for background 1 yd. narrow lace to frame Wallpaper paste Do-it-yourself fabric adhesive Clear all-purpose adhesive

Method: Trace the figures of the boy and girl once each, and the pretty maid three times (diagram 1) on to Vilene. Cut out very accurately, ignoring brim of boy's hat (diagram 2).

Begin with the boy. First cut a 1 inch square of pink twin-ply face tissue. Using wallpaper paste, stick the tissue so that it covers the face and overlaps all round it as diagram 3. Paste a piece of tissue over the hand in the same way. When quite dry, trim the tissue level with the cut edge of the Vilene, leaving that which overlaps the hair and sleeve.

Now cut a piece of black felt a little larger than his boot, and stick it over the Vilene (using fabric adhesive), so that the top edge slightly overlaps the bottom of his trousers. Turn the figure over and trim the felt level with the cut edge of the Vilene to the shape of his boot.

Returning to your master pattern – diagram 1 – trace a pattern for his trousers on to (preferably) tissue paper, extending it at the top to overlap the lower edge of his tunic (diagram 4). Cut the pattern out and pin it flat on to a piece of dark blue felt, then carefully cut it out. Fit the felt shape over your Vilene to make sure it is accurate before sticking it firmly into position.

Now trace a pattern for his tunic from diagram 1, *completely ignoring* his arm and collar (diagram 5). Cut this in mid-blue felt and stick to the Vilene. Next, trace a pattern for his collar – again ignoring the arm (diagram 6). Cut in white felt and stick down over the tunic. Finally, trace his arm, cut it in dark blue, like the trousers, and stick carefully into position.

Trace a pattern for his hair, allowing it to overlap the brim of the hat. I cut his hair in suede fabric, which gives it rather a suitable texture – but felt would do just as well. Stick this carefully into position over the face.

To make his straw boater, I plaited three strands of raffia. Knot them together at one end and make your plait. Cut a neatly plaited section 2 ins. long, quickly sealing the cut ends with fabric adhesive to prevent them becoming unplaited. Lay your Vilene figure over the master pattern (diagram 1), and stick the brim into position, overlapping each side as indicated. Make two more shorter lengths in the same way, and stick side-by-side to form crown of hat.

I trimmed the edge of his collar with a scrap of black ric-rac, and stuck the end of a tiny bit of Russian braid to the *back* of the Vilene figure, so that it stuck out at the front.

Mark a round dot for his eye in black ink.

Trace the figure of the little girl in diagram 1 on to Vilene in exactly the same way as you did for the boy (as instructed at the beginning). But now trace and cut *another* piece of Vilene the shape of the hand and lower part of the arm, following the broken line on the pattern (as in diagram 2).

Paste pink face tissue over the hand and arm, as for the boy, trimming level with the edge of the Vilene. Then stick a scrap of narrow lace over

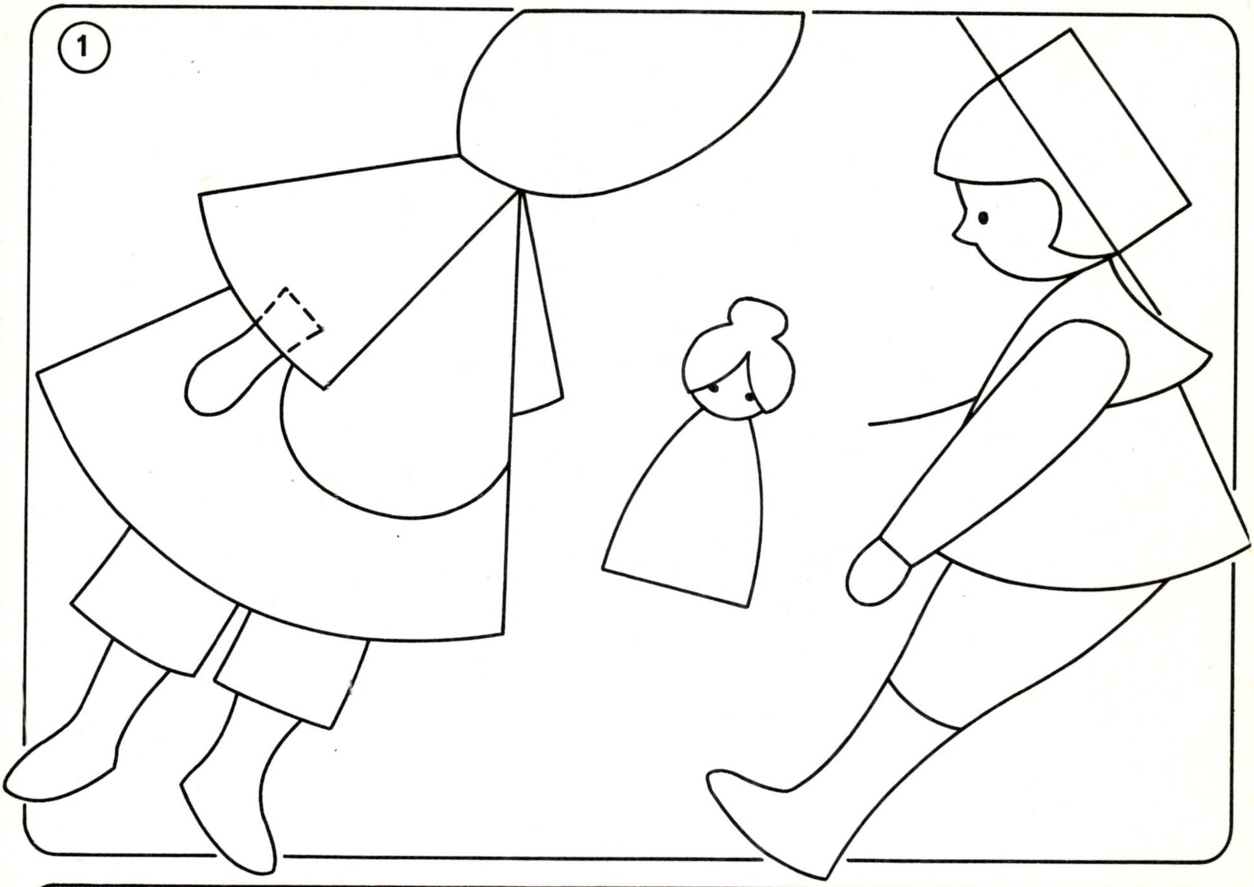
1

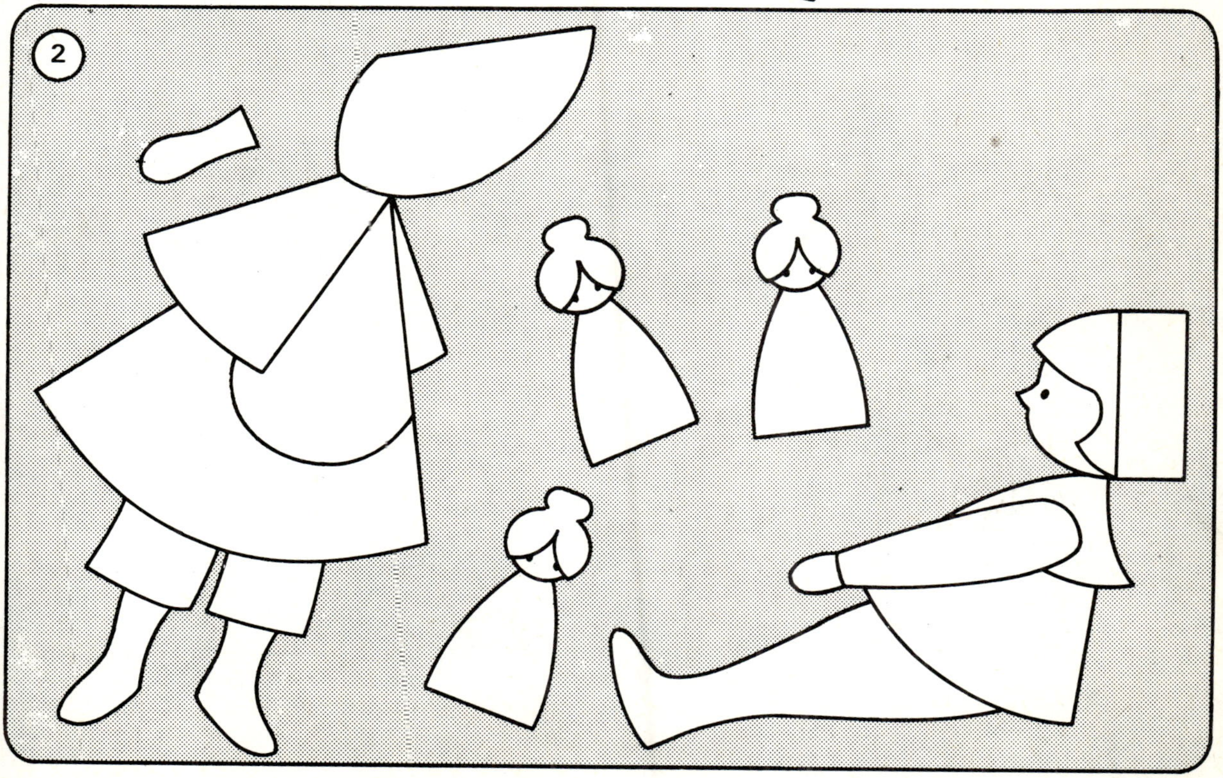
2

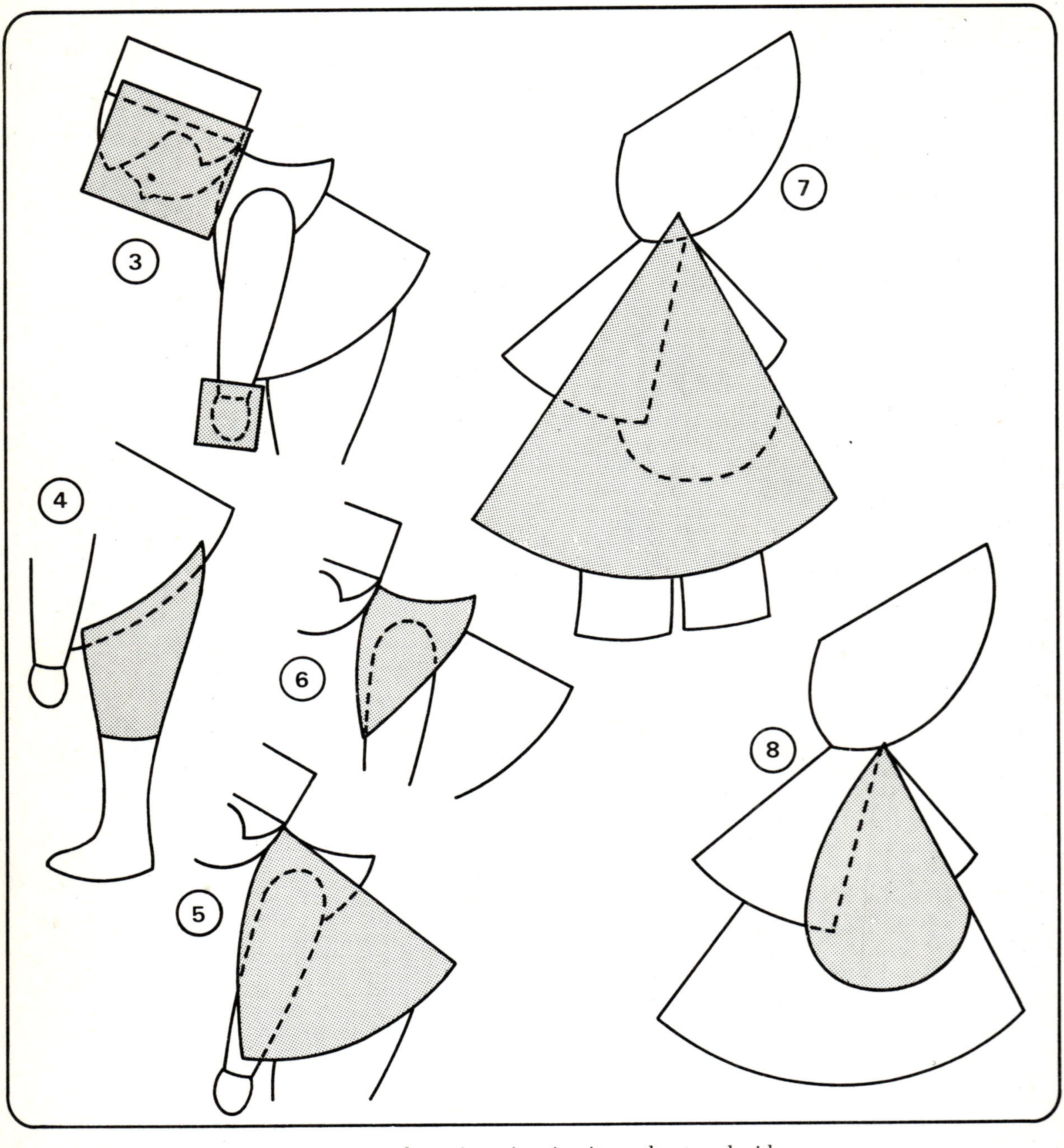

the wrist, trimming it neatly at each side.

Stick pieces of black felt to the Vilene for her boots, just as for the boy – *except* that the top edge of the felt should be level with the top of the boots. Trim the felt level with the edge of the Vilene.

Use the decorative edge of a scrap of broderie Anglaise or lace for her pantaloons, and this time allow the top edge to overlap the lower edge of her skirt a little.

Trace a pattern for her dress as diagram 7. Cut in fabric (or felt, if you prefer) and stick to the Vilene, trimming the edge neatly.

Trace a pattern for her pinafore as diagram 8. Try to fit the pattern to the design of a scrap of broderie Anglaise or lace – adapting the line of the lower edge slightly, if necessary. Stick into place, over the dress.

Now, following diagram 1, mark the position of the hand with pins, and then stick it into place.

Trace a pattern for the main half of the cape and cut in deep yellow felt: stick down over top of hand and edge of pinafore. Cover the Vilene for the other side of the cape as you did for the boots.

Trace a pattern for the bonnet and cut this in yellow felt too. But before sticking it to the Vilene, stick a little narrow lace to the *back* of the felt all round the front of the brim, so that the edge of the lace overlaps the edge of the felt. Now stick the felt to the Vilene – and stick some embroidered flowers or similar trimming on top, as illustrated.

Now your two main figures are complete, and you have only to make the three "pretty maids". Trace the master pattern in diagram 1 on to Vilene three times, and cut out, as instructed at the beginning. Paste tissue over the whole head of each, then trace a pattern for the hair and cut it in varying shades of felt for the three figures. Use lace or a dainty fabric for the dresses: I stuck two rows of $\frac{3}{4}$ in. deep lace over the Vilene for mine, trimming the sides level with the backing.

Mark two dots in black ink for the eyes.

You are now ready to assemble the picture, so it is necessary to decide on your background. I chose a soft mid-olive green felt, cut a square cake stand down to size to make a good, solid base. But a piece of stiff card, about 9 ins. deep by 12 ins. wide (the size of my picture) would do equally well. Stick the felt very smoothly to the board or card.

Now place your two figures on the felt background in the positions illustrated, with the three little maids in a row between. Add a line of shells (or sequins cut to shape – or coloured papers) just below the maids. Cut about seven random shapes in grey felt for the crazy-paving path, laying them on the felt below the shells.

Take about ten silver sequins or studs and place them above the maids for the bells, moving them around until you are satisfied with their positions. Finally, add lace or artificial flower-heads to complete the "garden", again moving them about to form an attractive arrangement.

When you are sure you are quite satisfied with the composition of your picture, you are ready to mount the various parts down.

Begin with the main figures. Lightly push pins into the felt to mark the position of the front and back points of the girl's bonnet, the corners of her cape, the corners of her skirt and the tips of her toes. Remove the figure and spread adhesive thoroughly all over the back. Then, beginning with the feet, carefully lower it into position on the felt between the pins, pressing it down firmly

Mark with pins each end of the brim of the boy's hat, the back corner of his tunic, the tip of his hand and the toe and heel of his boot. Spread adhesive over the back of the figure as before, but *omit the hand* – and also the overlapping Russian braid at the front. Stick down into position, then stick a flower under his hand, as illustrated, before sticking the hand and overlapping braid neatly into place.

Mark and stick the three maids in the same way.

Use a clear, all-purpose adhesive to stick the shells firmly to the background, and also the silver sequins, or studs. When you have done this, stick a tiny seed pearl below each silver "bell" for the clapper.

Finally, using fabric adhesive again, stick the path and the flowers into place, to complete the picture.

I "framed" my collage with narrow cream lace, which I stuck down with double-sided tape.

3 Developing the detail

Already, in only your second collage, you saw how the simple shape of the girl's bonnet was decorated with lace and embroidery, the boy's collar trimmed with braid – and the garden filled in with flowers. That was just an example of how collage invites the addition of detailed decoration. Begin with a simple design, and then use it as a vehicle for a selection from your hoard of ribbon, braid, lace and so on.

The two subjects in this chapter – although they are so completely different – are designed specifically to give you this opportunity. The happy little Red Indians are fringed, braided, beaded and feathered – whilst their wigwam must be the gayest in the reservation! Little touches like the wisp of cotton wool smoke, and the tufts of guipure lace grass are the kind of thing which make an attractive collage complete. The Edwardian lady emphasises the use of fabric and lace to create a delicate and elegant fashion plate figure. In contrast to the colourful Red Indians, the colour scheme is muted and subtle, adding to the sophistication of the design. But once again she offers ample scope for trimming with odd bits of lace, braid, ribbon and flowers. One of the interesting details to note is the treatment of the hair in both collages.

Remember that part of the fascination of collage is examining the finished picture to see how different effects have been achieved. It is a challenge to the imagination to use materials and methods which create as realistic an effect as possible.

Red Indians at Home

Illustrated in colour on page 20

Choose strong, bright colours for this collage, to give a feeling of sunshine and warmth. The design illustrates the advantages of making up your pieces separately on a Vilene backing: there are no untidy cut ends of trimming visible – all the raw ends are taken neatly round and stuck to the back of the Vilene.

The Red Indians' hair is a development on the previous chapter, too. It is carefully built up with strands of knitting wool (although you can use felt if you prefer, of course): I used double-sided tape for this job – but fabric adhesive would do.

Materials:

- Medium-weight Vilene or Pellon
- Felt in orange, gold, light brown, brown, dark brown and bright green
- Assorted braids, embroidered ribbons, lace and similar trimmings
- Narrow silk fringe (brown and yellow)
- 3- or 4-ply brown knitting wool
- Tiny coloured beads
- 2 coloured feathers
- Pink twin-ply face tissue

(Right) Mr. Woo – the colourful owl
(Below) Mary, Mary, Quite Contrary

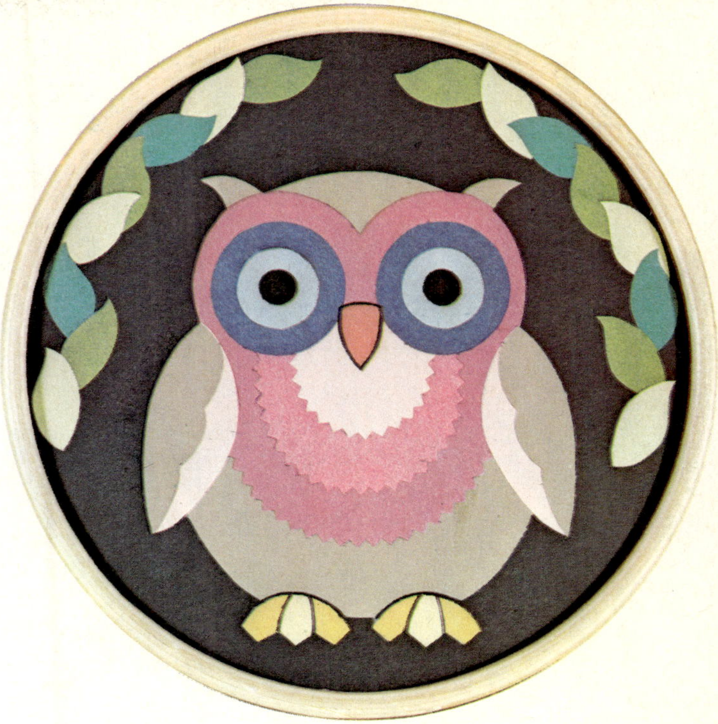

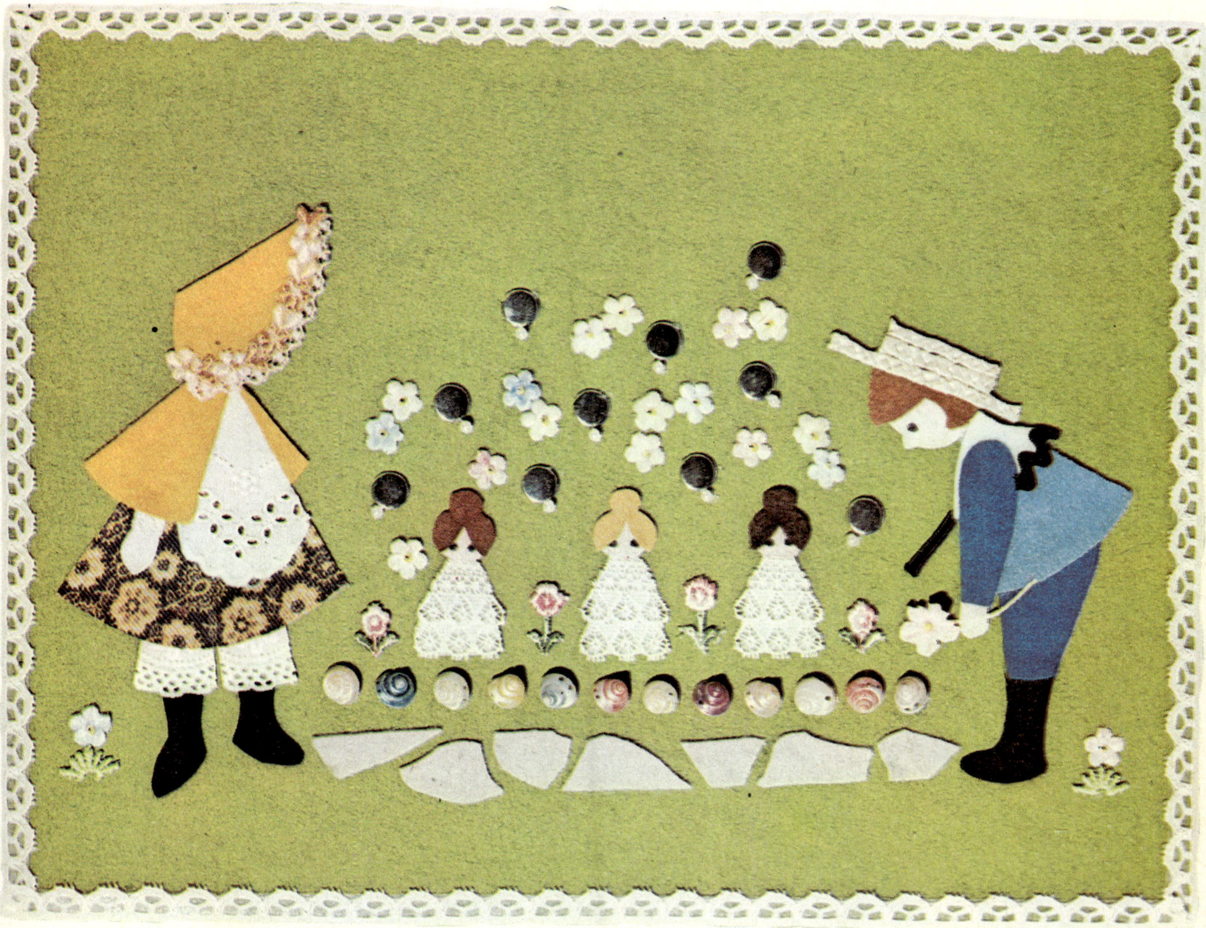

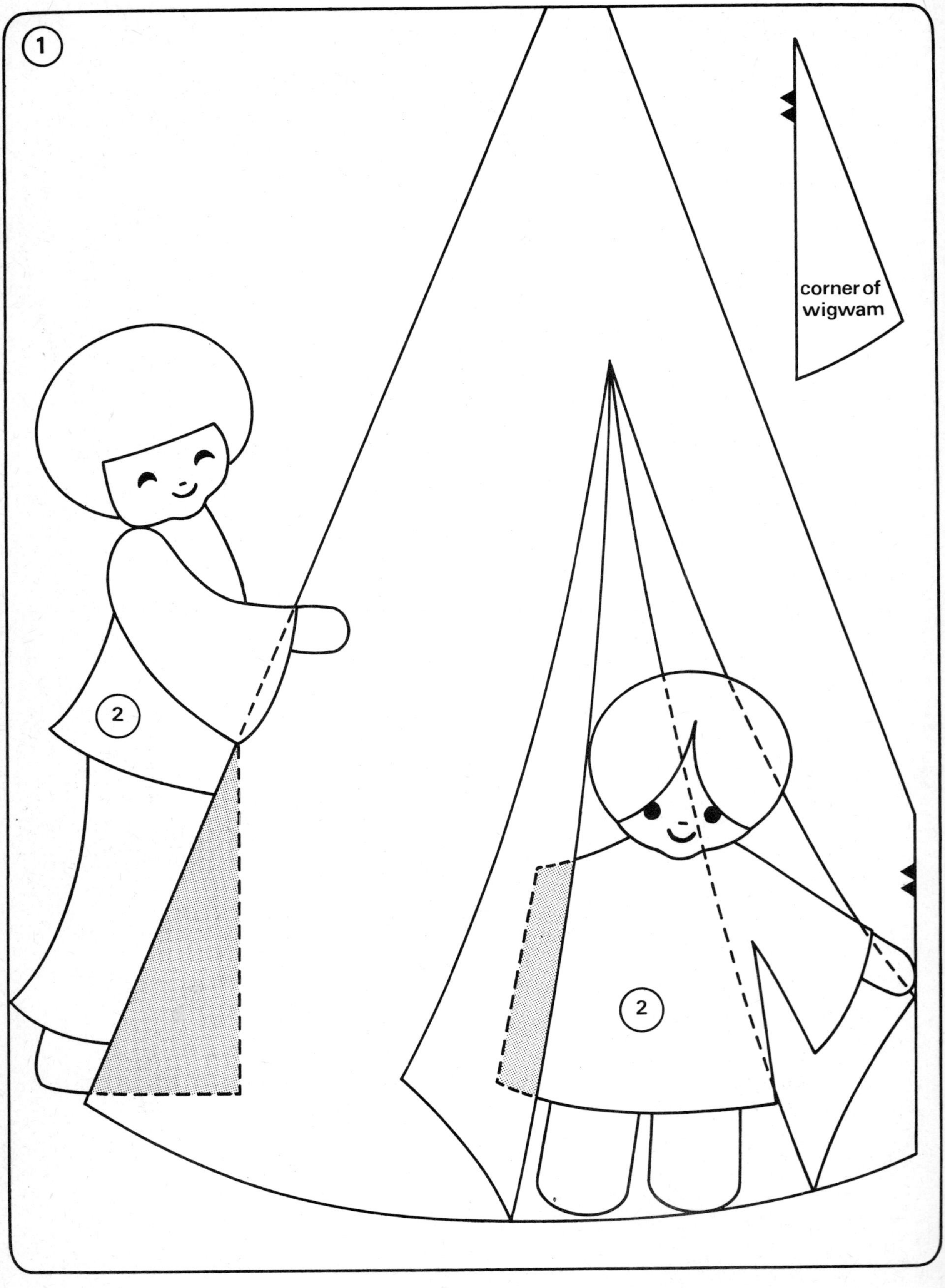
1
corner of wigwam
2
2

Materials: (cont.)

Green guipure lace daisies (or alternative)
2 wooden cocktail sticks
Cotton wool
12 in. square cake stand or piece of stiff card
Felt or fabric for the background
$1\frac{1}{2}$ yds. contrasting braid to frame
Double-sided tape (optional)
Wallpaper paste
Do-it-yourself fabric adhesive
Clear all-purpose adhesive

Method: Trace the wigwam on to Vilene, following the lines of the flaps and ignoring the broken lines and shaded areas indicating the figures. Trace the two figures from page 18 on to Vilene too, as in the last chapter, including the shaded areas which will eventually be hidden by the wigwam. Cut out.

Paste twin-ply pink face tissue over the faces and hands as before. When dry, trim edges and then mark hairlines softly in pencil. If using double-sided tape, cover the whole hair area with tape. Otherwise use fabric adhesive – a small section at a time. Begin with the boy – starting at the inner left-hand side of his face (see the arrows in diagram 3). Lay a strand of wool on top of the tape, overlapping the edge of the head about $\frac{1}{2}$ in. above and below. Lay another strand of wool as close as possible to the first, again overlapping at top and bottom. Continue in this way, working outwards, until the side of the head is reached. Now make the fringe in the same way, beginning next to the first strand – but this time placing the cut edge of each new strand of wool level with the lower edge of the fringe, though still overlapping the top. Complete the right-hand side of the head as the left. Now take all the strands overlapping the *top* of the head neatly over and stick to the back of the Vilene. Trim all the "hair" overlapping the lower edge level with the Vilene, using a sharp pair of scissors.

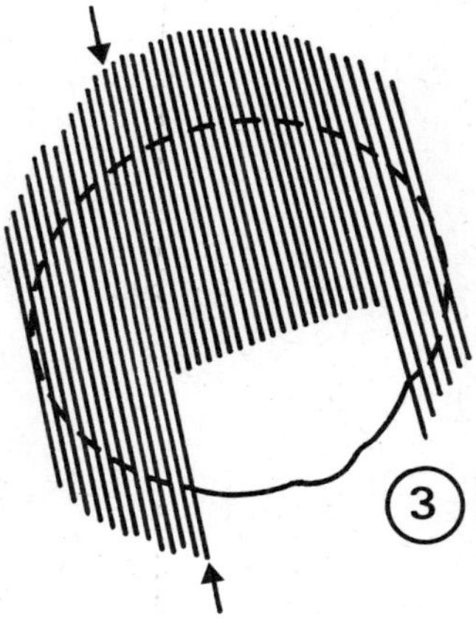

3

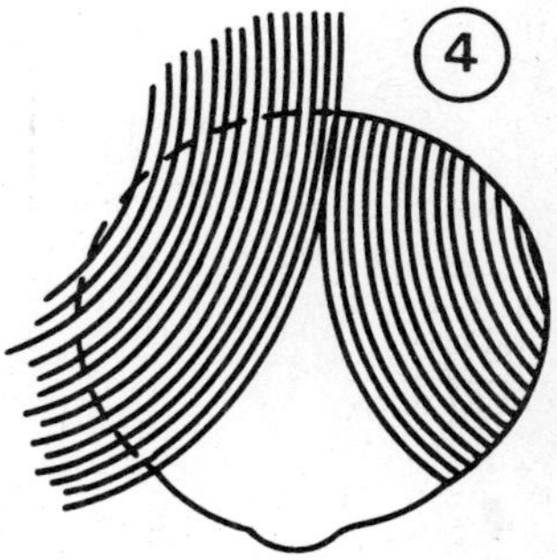

4

Make the girl's hair in the same way, beginning at the inner edge against the face, this time curving the wool round to follow the line of the hair – and overlapping the strands above and below. Complete one side at a time, working outwards until the edge of the head is reached. Then stick *all* the ends, above *and* below, round to the back of the Vilene (diagram 4).

To dress the boy, cover his shoe with dark brown felt, as for the boy in Chapter 1, allowing the felt to overlap the edge of the trousers, and the shaded area at the side.

Trace a pattern for his trousers, overlapping the lower edge of his tunic and the broken line at the side. Cut in brown felt and then stick the top edge of a piece of fringe to the *back* of the lower edge. Trim so that a bare $\frac{1}{4}$ in. overlaps the edge of the trousers, then stick them into position. Trim with braid, as illustrated.

Trace a pattern for the tunic, ignoring the arm. Cut in light brown felt and trim the lower edge with fringe, as for the trousers, before sticking into place.

Trace the arm, cut in brown, as the trousers, trim the sleeve edge with fringe and then stick carefully into position.

I cut the same narrow braid I used for the trousers in half to trim the edge of the sleeve and tunic: allow the cut ends to overlap the edge of the felt and stick them neatly round to the back of the Vilene.

Stick a narrow band of ribbon or braid across his head, sticking the overlapping ends to the back, then stick a small feather to the back of

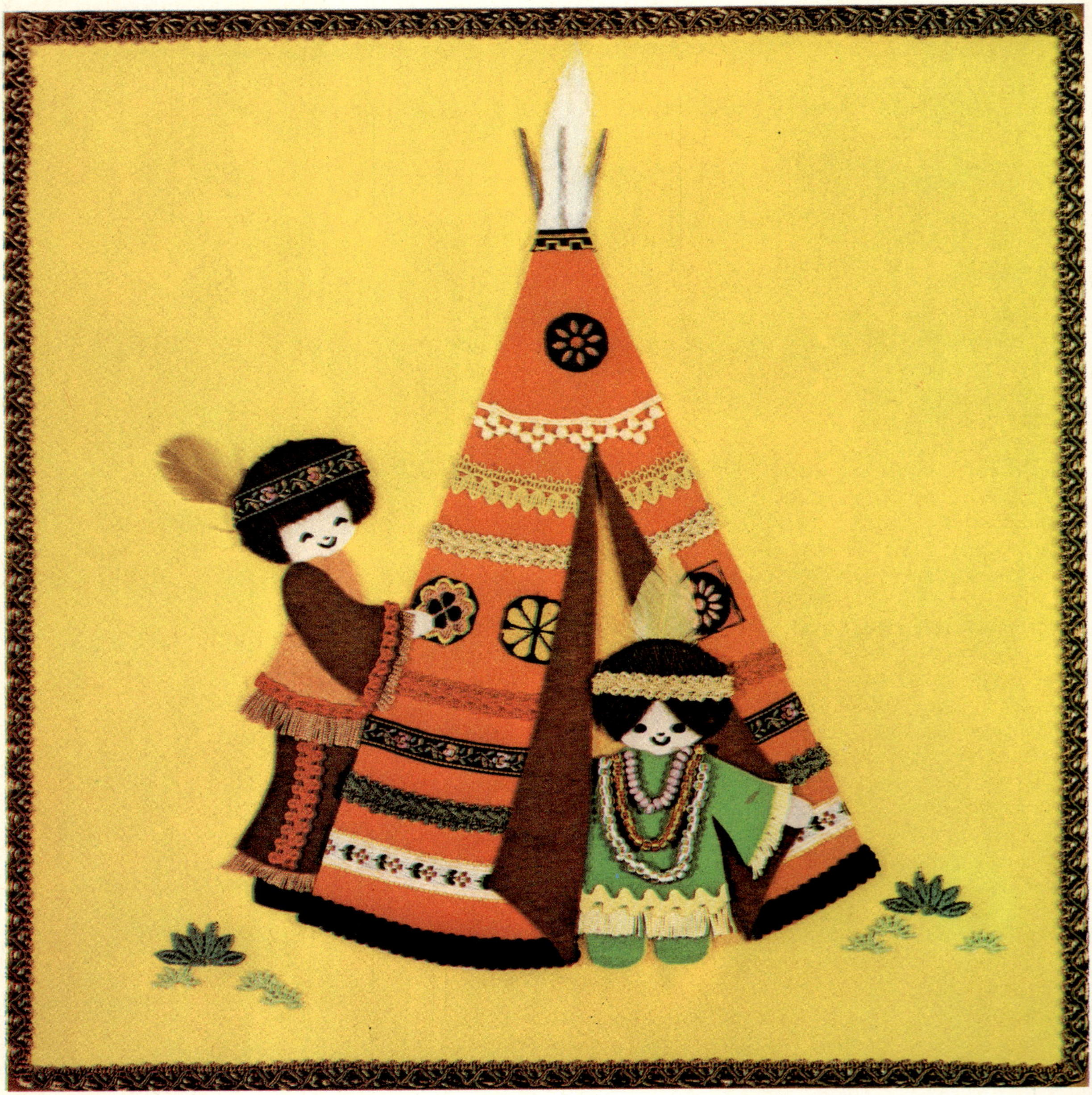

(Above) Red Indians at Home
(Opposite) Edwardiana

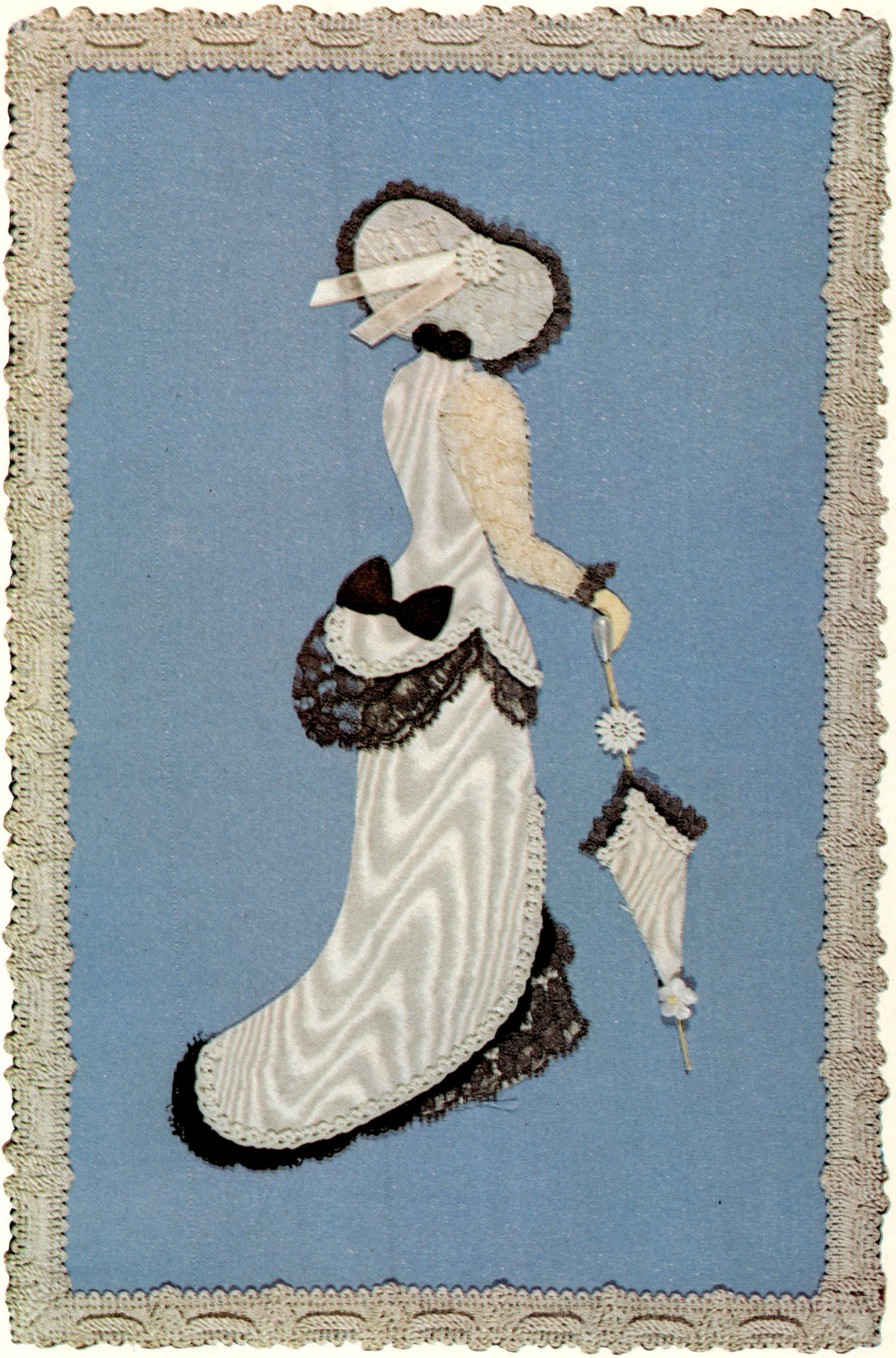

the head so that it protrudes at the angle illustrated.

Begin with the girl's legs. Cover her two "knees" with green felt so that it overlaps the lower edge of the tunic.

Trace a pattern for her tunic, including the shaded area beyond the broken line. Cut in the same green felt, then trim the sleeve and lower edge with fringe as for the boy. I added a row of ric-rac along the lower edge, too. Stick the tunic into position, then stitch strings of tiny coloured beads at each shoulder, as illustrated.

Stick a narrow band round her head, and add a central feather (trimmed to size and shape if necessary), as for the boy.

Trace a pattern for the "inside" of the wigwam – between the flaps – allowing it to overlap the edge of the flaps at each side. Cut in gold felt and stick into place on the Vilene.

Trace a pattern for the wigwam itself, *including* the flaps. Cut this in orange felt, cutting away the centre division. Stick to the Vilene. Now stick rows of narrow braid, ribbon, lace, etcetera, all the way up the wigwam, following the curved shape of the lower edge. Stick the cut edge of the trimming level with the edge of the centre division, but allow to overlap the edge of the felt at each side, taking round and sticking neatly to the back of the Vilene. Add motifs higher up, as illustrated: I cut mine from a scrap of wider embroidered ribbon.

Trace patterns for the flaps and cut them in brown. Stick the *right-hand* one only into position, covering the cut ends of the rows of trimming.

Now stick the girl carefully into position, overlapping the sides of the centre division as indicated in diagram 1. Then complete with the left-hand flap, over the side of the girl's tunic.

Position the boy as indicated in diagram 1, then stick the lower half of the figure behind the wigwam, with the hand in front, as illustrated.

Cover a cake stand, or 12 inch square of stiff card, with felt for the background (I used a bright yellow). Then place the completed wigwam and figures about $1\frac{1}{4}$ ins. above the lower edge, and move it about until you are satisfied.

Mark the position very carefully with pins, as in Chapter 1, then remove the whole section and spread adhesive over the back of the Vilene – leaving about 1 inch free at the top of the wigwam (ignore feather and fringe). Stick carefully back into position, pressing down into place.

Draw in the children's features very carefully in black.

Break two cocktail sticks in half and colour three of the pieces dark brown with paint or crayon. Then stick two in a V shape, the broken ends under the top of the wigwam, extending above as illustrated (use clear all-purpose adhesive for this). Stick a wisp of cotton wool between the sticks, extending slightly above, then stick the final piece of cocktail stick vertically in the centre of the V, over the cotton wool. Stick down the top of the wigwam.

Cut green lace daisies in half, or indicate tufts of grass with an alternative trimming or green raffia, etcetera, and stick at each side, following the illustration.

Finally, stick braid all round the edge to frame.

Edwardiana

Illustrated in colour on page 21

Coffee and cream are my choice for a sophisticated colour scheme: you will no doubt have other ideas of your own. As with the previous collage, a simple basic design relies on trimmings and decoration for its effect. But in this case a striking fabric is used and the decoration is as delicate as possible. And in a different way you will appreciate the necessity of working your collage on Vilene, only to be mounted down at the very end.

Materials:

- Medium-weight Vilene or Pellon
- Cream moiré or alternative fabric or wide ribbon
- Cream lace
- Brown lace
- Black lace
- Narrow cream braid
- Brown satin fabric or ribbon
- Narrow cream ribbon
- Lace or artificial flowers
- Dark brown stranded embroidery cotton
- Scrap of chamois or kid
- Drop pearl or small bead
- Very thin stick (split bamboo or similar strip)
- 14 in. square cake stand, or stiff card 14 in. by 9 in.
- Light blue fabric for the background
- $1\frac{1}{2}$ yds. contrasting braid to frame
- Double-sided tape
- Firm adhesive tape
- Wallpaper paste
- Do-it-yourself fabric adhesive
- Clear all-purpose adhesive

Method: Trace the figure (ignoring the broken lines) – and also the parasol (ignoring the stick) – in diagram 1 on to Vilene and cut out. Now carefully cut the figure in half along the lower edge of the bodice between points A–B, and then cut the skirt section between points C–D, so that the front skirt and back train are separate. Trace the arm – ending at the wrist – on to Vilene again (diagram 2), and also the hat, and cut these out too.

Trace a pattern for the bodice, following the broken line running through the arm (diagram 3). Cut in fabric: if using moiré or a similar material, position your pattern so that the grain runs in the direction of the body, as illustrated. Also, if you are using any silky fabric which tends to fray, cut the piece slightly larger than the pattern all the way round. Stick to figure and trim level with Vilene.

Stick a tiny piece of chamois or kid over her hand, then trim to the shape of the Vilene.

Trace a pattern and cut fabric for the sleeve, then stick to the *separate* Vilene for the arm. Cover this with a layer of toning lace, and trim both fabrics level with the Vilene. Finally, stick a scrap of brown lace behind the wrist edge so that it overlaps to form a frill, as illustrated. Now stick the completed sleeve into position over the arm on the main figure.

Trace a pattern for the lace falling below the bustle, following the broken lines in diagram 1. Cut in brown lace and stick behind the

The Houses on the Hill

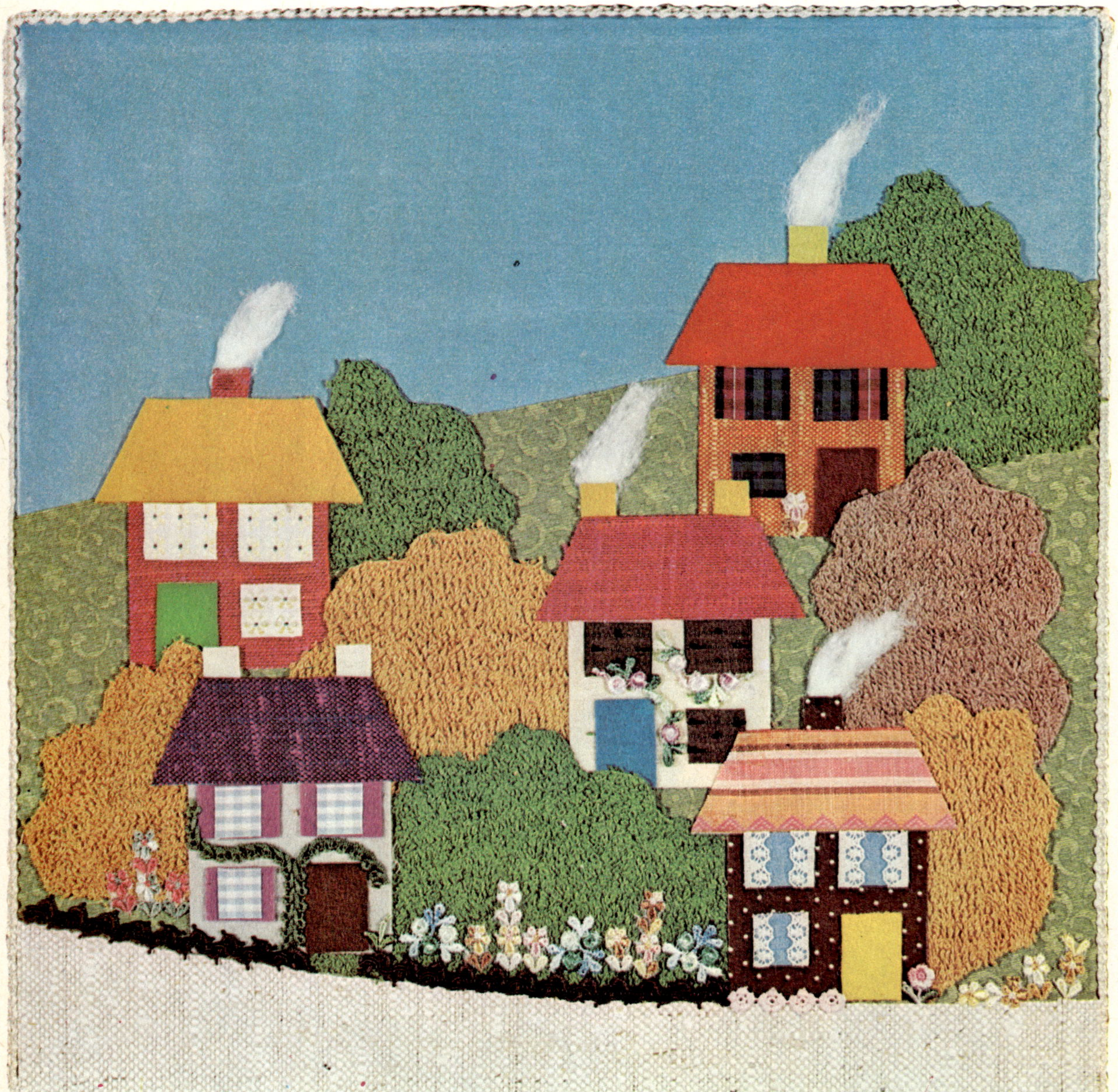

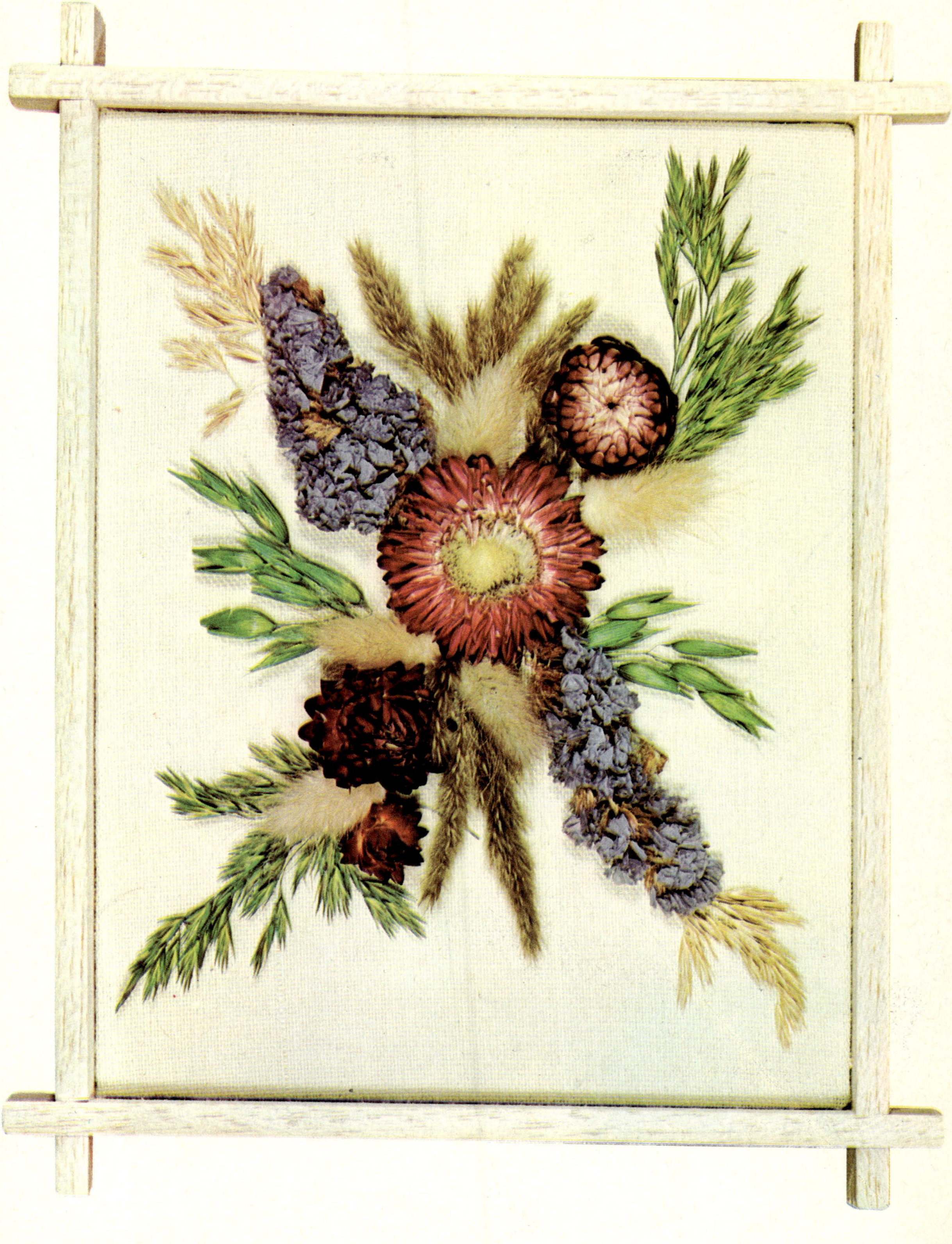

Summer Garden

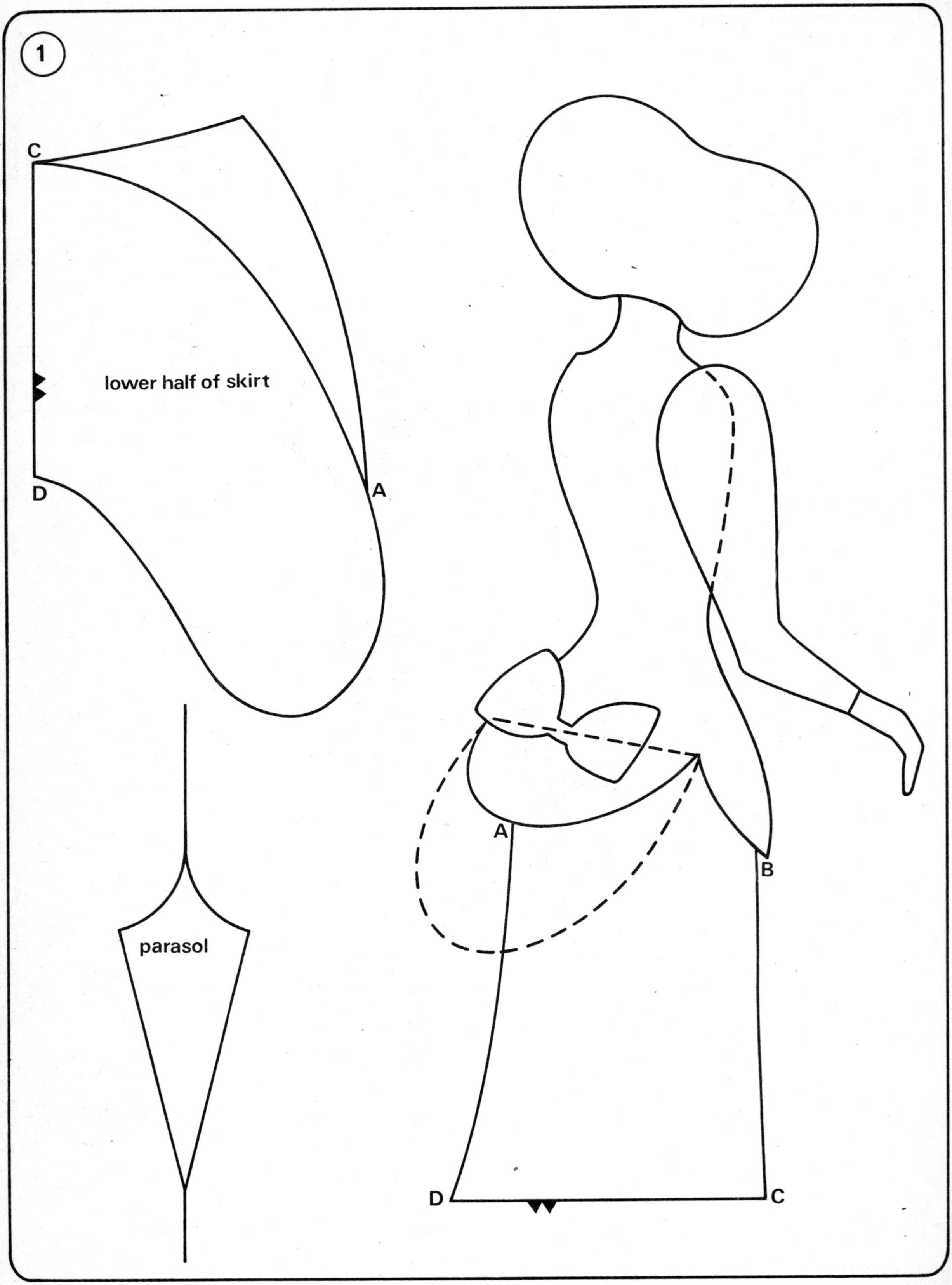
1
C
lower half of skirt
D
A
parasol
A
B
D
C

Vilene, placing both lace and Vilene over diagram 1 for accurate positioning.

Stick another scrap of brown lace behind the apron front, following the illustration.

Trace the bow and then, if using satin – which frays easily – stick the un-cut tracing to the dull back of the fabric and then cut the bow out through both paper and fabric: this will ensure clean, sharp edges. Stick carefully into position. I cut a narrow cream silk braid in half down the centre to trim the lower edge of the bustle and apron.

Trace a pattern for the main skirt section and cut in fabric as for the bodice, trimming the edge neatly when you have stuck it to the Vilene. Cover the tiny front skirt section with fabric, too. Then stick brown lace over the fabric, allowing it to overlap the front edge slightly in "frills", as illustrated: leave an area of lace overlapping the curved line C–D.

Border the lower edge of the train with black lace as illustrated: I used a scalloped lace, cutting it into pieces and sticking each scallop separately to the back of the Vilene round the sharp curve at the end of the train. I found double-sided tape made this job much easier, as you can keep lifting the lace until it is just as you want it. Cut the tape into narrow strips and stick round the edge of the back of the Vilene.

Now fit the lace-covered front skirt section neatly back into place against the main skirt, and stick the overlapping lace to the back of the Vilene to hold it in position.

Trim the edge of the train with narrow silk braid as the bodice, following the illustration.

Now place the two halves right side down on a flat surface, and fit the bodice and skirt together, matching the cut edges between A–B exactly. Join with small pieces of adhesive tape.

Cover the separate hat shape with fabric, then with toning lace. Edge narrowly with brown lace, stuck to the back of the Vilene (I used double-sided tape again) – leaving the lower edge untrimmed. Stick the hat to the Vilene figure, then add narrow ribbons and a flower to trim, as illustrated. You will realise that it is not strictly necessary to make the hat separately – but I found it easier.

Take a 12 in. length of stranded embroidery cotton and saturate it in wallpaper paste. Then wrap it tightly round the tip of your index finger, lift gently off and then twist the resulting circle into a figure 8 shape (diagram 4). Add more wallpaper paste before leaving to dry, and then stick at nape of neck, over top of bodice and just below brim of hat.

I used a thin strip of cane from a bamboo table mat for the handle of her parasol – but a cocktail stick, or any other thin stick would do. Cover the Vilene with fabric, then trim the top with lace and braid as illustrated. Stick the handle behind the Vilene, extending $\frac{3}{4}$ in. below the bottom point: shape this end to a point with a sharp knife. Decorate with flowers as illustrated.

Cut a cake stand to measure 14 ins. by 9 ins., or use stiff card. Cover with felt or fabric for the background. Then place the figure on it, moving it and the parasol around until you are quite satisfied with the position and arrangement. Mark with pins and then stick the figure down. Stick the drop pearl or bead inside her hand to act as the parasol handle: then cut the stick to length and stick into place below the pearl.

Stick braid all round the edge to frame.

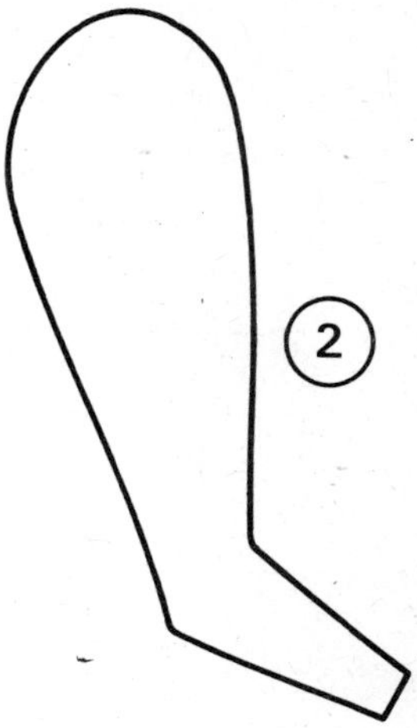

2

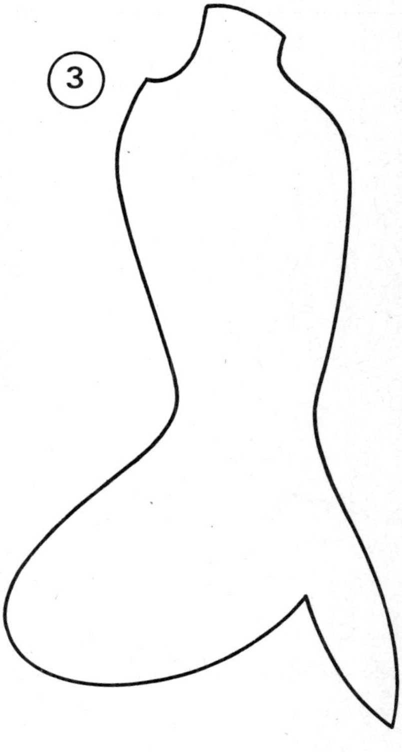

3

4

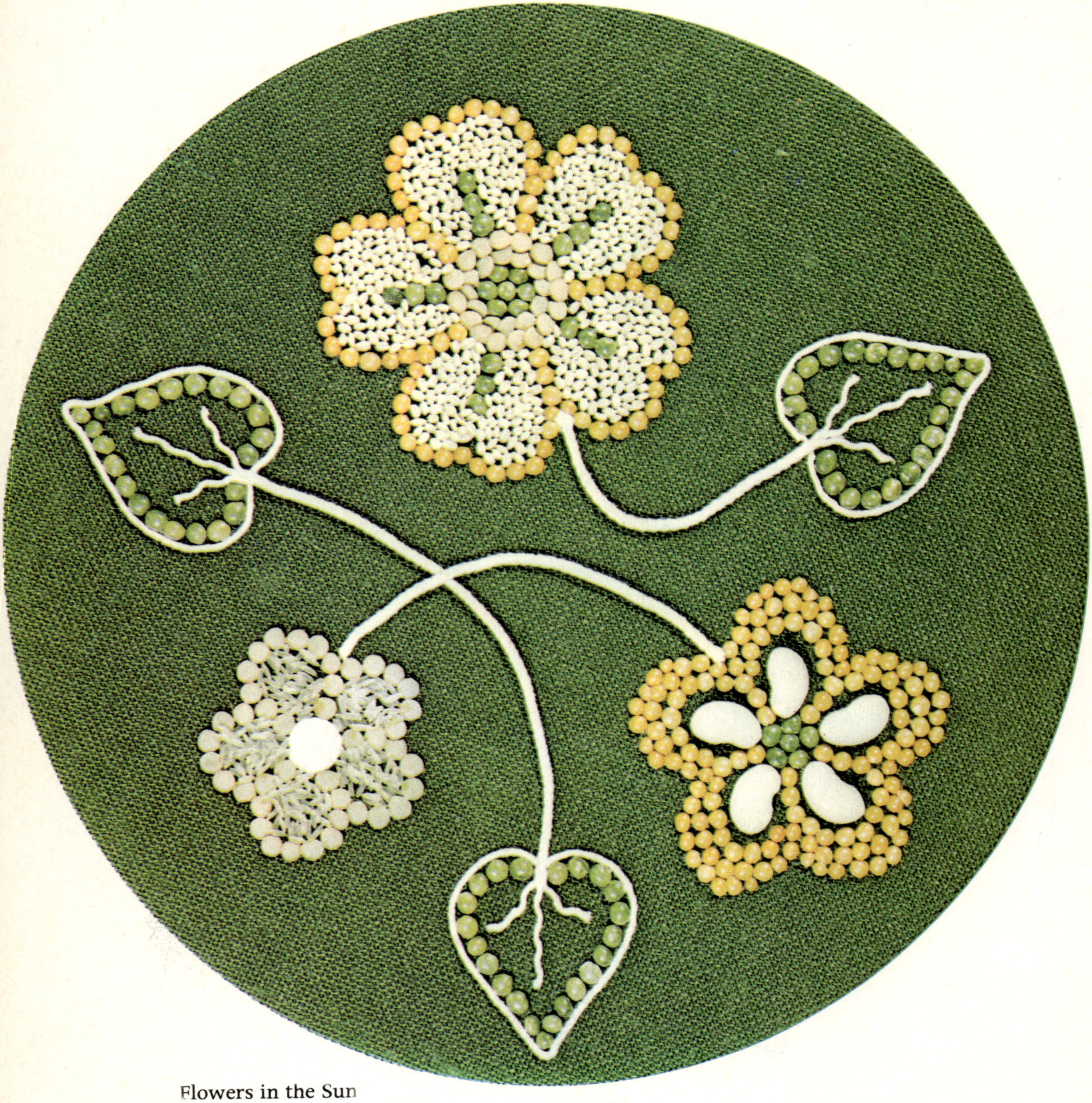

Flowers in the Sun

Roedd Iesu ar ei ffordd i Gapernaum yng nghwch pysgota Simon Pedr. Erbyn iddynt gyrraedd y lan yr oedd tyrfa fawr o bobl ar y traeth. Roedd llawer ohonynt yn gloff, dall neu wedi bod yn sâl ers amser maith ac yn credu y medrai Iesu eu gwella.

Safodd yr Iesu yn ymyl y cwch a daeth gŵr ato a dweud,

"Mae fy merch fach yn sâl. Bron â marw. Tyrd ar unwaith i'w gwella. Brysia."

I ffwrdd â'r Iesu gyda'r gŵr o'r enw Jairus. Fel yr oeddynt yn cyrraedd y tŷ rhedodd rhywun atynt a dweud bod yr hogan fach wedi marw. Ymlaen aeth yr Iesu a phan welodd yr hogan fach dywedodd.

"Peidiwch â chadw sŵn, cysgu yn drwm mae'r hogan fach."

Doedd neb yn ei gredu ac anfonodd yr Iesu yr holl bobl swnllyd allan o'r tŷ. Yna, dywedodd yr Iesu, "Cod fy merch." Agorodd y ferch ei llygaid ac edrych o'i chwmpas. Cododd ar ei heistedd, yna allan â hi o'r gwely a rhedeg o gwmpas.

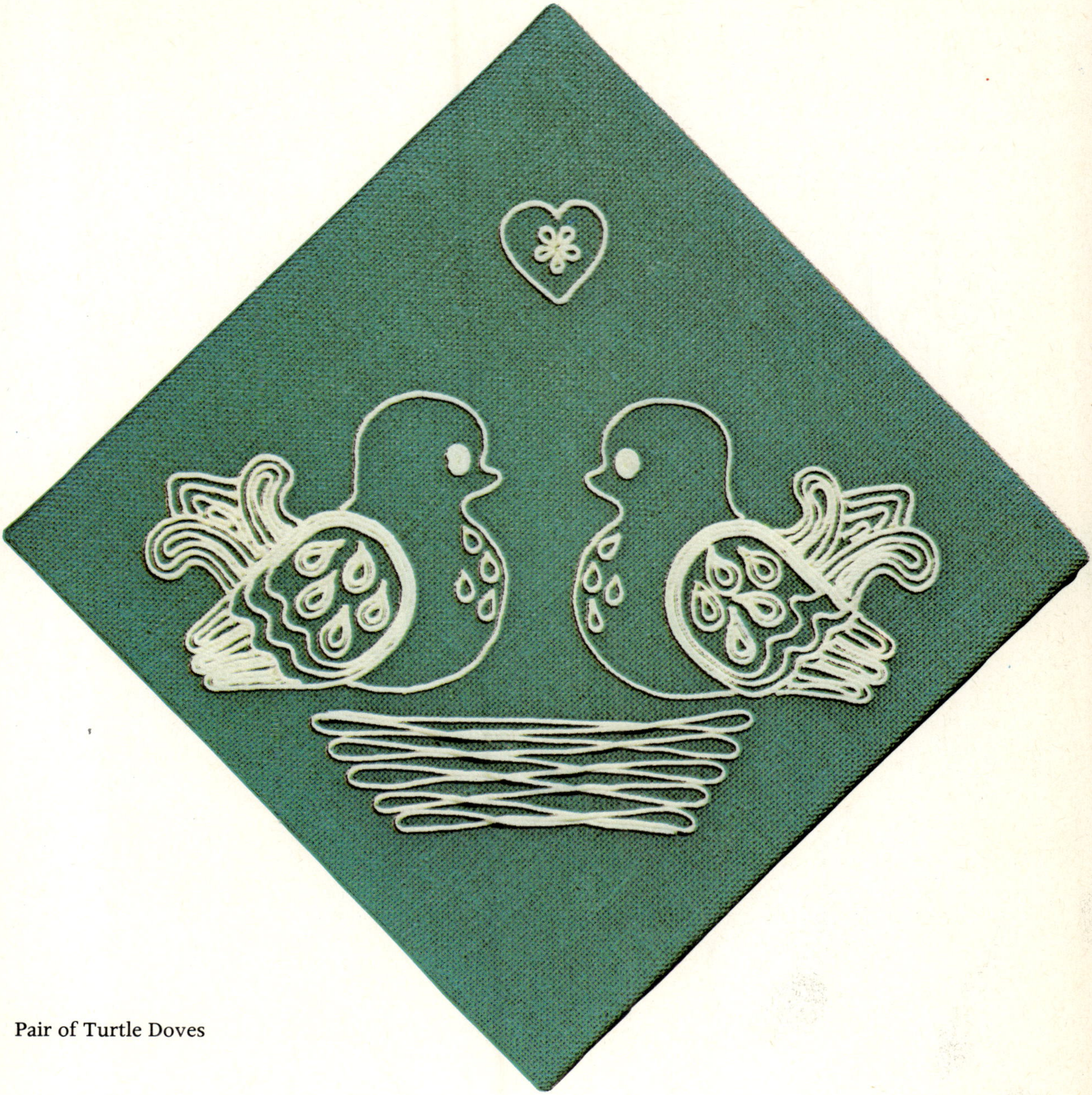

Pair of Turtle Doves

4 Composing a picture

This chapter gives you the opportunity for even greater freedom of expression. For the first design, you take a very simple basic house and create five – or as many as you please – completely different versions. Then you put them together in an arrangement of your own choosing, filling in the details to unite them and complete the picture. You can follow my version as much or as little as you wish.

The second design offers you freedom of choice in another way. It combines a very wide variety of materials, and allows you to exercise your own initiative in substituting effective alternatives – and again re-arranging the positioning – to make your collage completely individual.

Both these collages are a logical development of the various techniques you have learned from the designs in chapters 1 and 2. You will find exactly the same methods are employed, making these compositions no more difficult than the previous examples.

The Houses on the Hill

Illustrated in colour on page 24

Here is a full description of how I created **my** picture. But your version can vary as much as you please: obviously your materials will be different – but you can compose a completely different arrangement, too.

Materials:

Medium-weight Vilene or Pellon
Assorted dress and furnishing fabrics, and felts – patterned, woven and plain
Green, gold and brown towelling – or alternative rough fabrics for bushes and trees
Light blue satin (or alternative) for the sky
Mid-green cotton (or alternative) for the hill
Coarsely woven natural linen or hessian for the road
Narrow braids, lace and embroidered or artificial flowers to decorate
Cotton wool
12 inch square cake stand or stiff card
$1\frac{1}{2}$ yds. woven braid to edge
Wallpaper paste
Do-it-yourself fabric adhesive

Method: For each house, trace the outline from diagram 1 on to Vilene, and cut out: cut some with a central chimney and others with one at each side.

Cover the walls of the house with felt or fabric, allowing the top edge to overlap the lower edge of the roof. Choose a light or dark colour, but avoid greens.

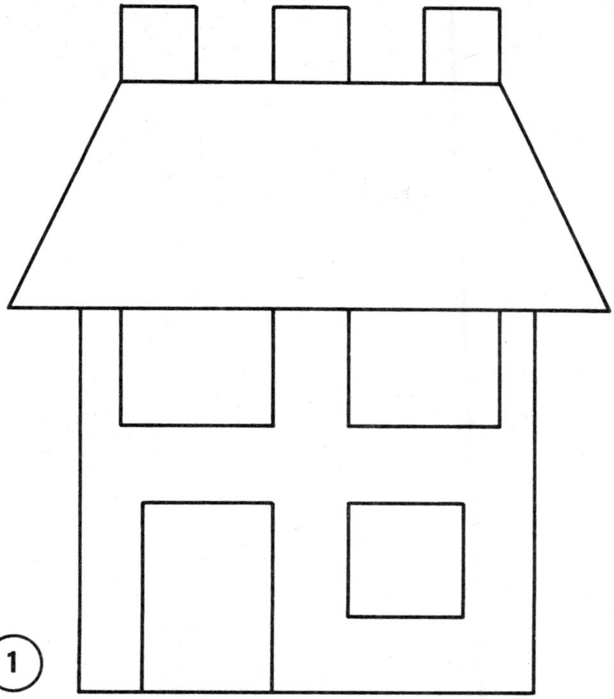

1

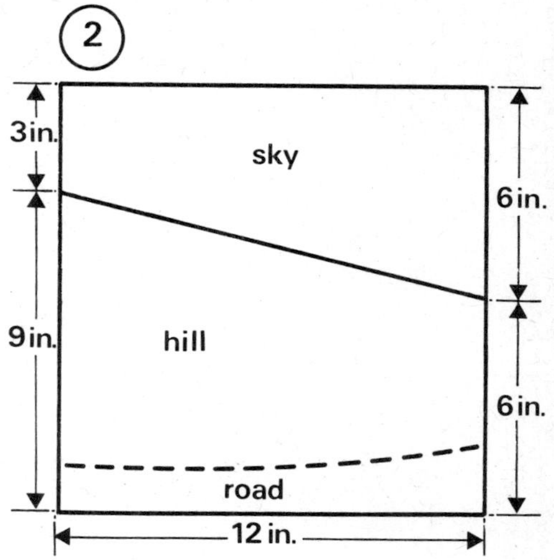

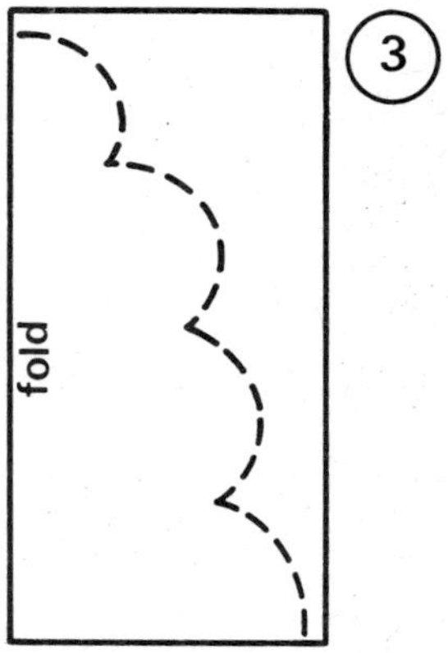

Cover the chimneys, letting this overlap the roof too.

Trace a pattern for the roof, or trace it on to Vilene, and cut in felt or fabric. I found it more satisfactory to mount fabric on to a separate Vilene roof before mounting it down on the house itself: but felt can go straight down. Again, choose a colour that will stand out well against green or blue.

Trace a pattern for an upper window, one for the lower window and one for the door. Cut the windows in felt or fabric: I used part of a tartan design for one house, tiny woven flowered dress fabric for another, some brown and black woven cotton for the third, blue felt bordered by narrow lace curtains, and finally, blue check gingham mounted on mauve felt cut slightly wider than the window pattern to form shutters.

I cut all my front doors in felt, as this gave a bold effect and a strong, contrasting colour for each house.

Stick the windows and doors into position, reversing the arrangement of the lower window and door on half the houses.

Stick braid "creeper" or flowers to the walls of some houses, as illustrated (or leave this until later, if you prefer).

For an arrangement similar to mine, rule a line across a 12 inch square cake stand, or piece of stiff card, as diagram 2.

Using wallpaper paste, stick blue satin smoothly over the top section of the board, overlapping the pencil line: take the edges of the fabric over the sides and top of the board, mitring the corners, and stick neatly to the back.

I used a mid-green dress cotton with a faint printed pattern for the hill. Stick the straight cut edge level with the pencil line on the board, finishing the side and bottom edges neatly as before.

Cut a strip of coarsely woven linen or hessian for the road – the same length as the base of the picture, but sloping gently from $1\frac{1}{4}$ inches at one side to 2 inches at the other. Stick at the base of the board, over the green cotton.

Bedtime Story

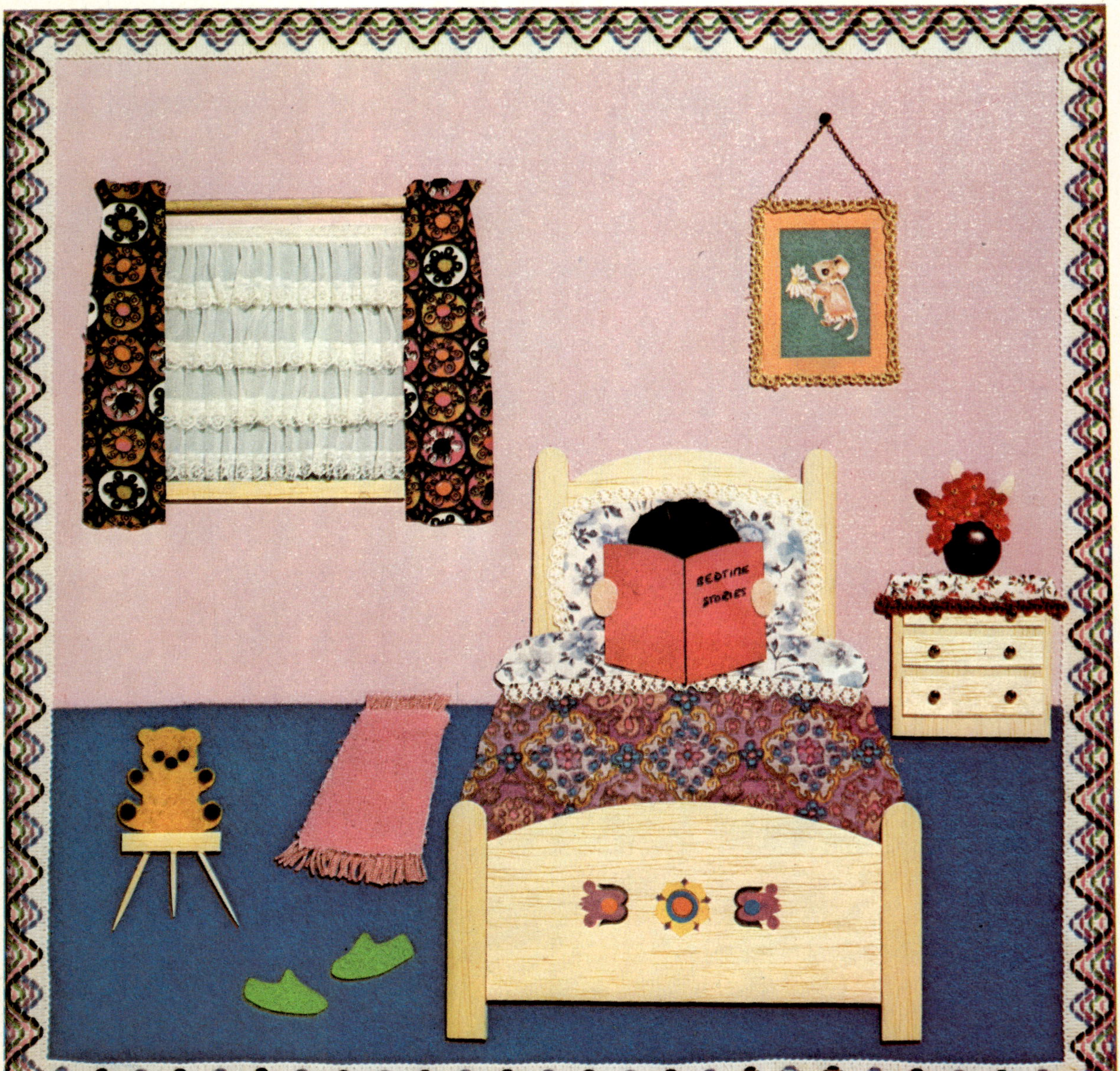

When the background is quite dry, arrange your houses on the hill. My two lowest houses are each 2 inches from the side edge – overlapping the upper ones as illustrated.

Now cut bushes and trees freehand from coloured towelling: cut a piece of towelling slightly larger than the size you want your bush or tree to be. Fold it in half vertically, and then cut a random scalloped shape through the double fabric, as diagram 3. Open out and place in position – under and over the houses, and overlapping other trees or bushes as illustrated. If you find it easier, sketch a pattern for the shape you require on a piece of tissue paper placed over the arrangement. Then use this to cut the exact shape you want in towelling.

When you are quite satisfied with the composition of your picture, begin to mount the separate pieces down, beginning at the back – but being sure to mark carefully with pins (or pencil dots) the positions of any overlapping pieces which have to be moved. Try to move only those pieces which overlap the actual item you are sticking down: if you work in this way you will be able to stick each piece down in order without losing your original arrangement – ending with the lowest houses. *Do not stick the chimneys down yet.*

Border the edge of the road with fancy braid, and stick an assortment of lace, embroidered and artificial flowers along the front, as illustrated.

Finally, stick wisps of cotton wool coming out of some of the chimneys (all curling in the same direction!), and then stick all the chimneys down into place.

Stick braid round the sides of the picture, to form a frame, as illustrated.

Bedtime Story

Illustrated in colour opposite

Here is a series of separate items which build up to make a complete picture – and an opportunity to combine scraps of patterned fabric to create a pleasing effect. Always try to keep a colour scheme at the back of your mind, so that you don't end up with a complete hotch-potch of totally unrelated colours. This can spoil an otherwise clever composition.

Incidentally, I wanted to use paper for the walls to make them realistic – proper wallpaper, if possible. But I just couldn't find the colour I wanted. I hope you will be luckier – but I solved my problem by substituting fine poplin dress cotton in just the right shade: this is a trick I often find useful, and worth remembering.

Materials:

Medium-weight Vilene or Pellon
White cartridge paper
Plain paper or fabric for walls (15 ins. by 9 ins.)
Plain felt or fabric for the floor (14 ins. by 5 ins.)
Patterned fabrics for pillow and sheet, coverlet, curtains and tablecloth
Scrap of towelling for the rug
Scraps of gold, black and brown felt for bear
Scrap of felt for slippers
Mid-blue coloured paper for window, and bright colours for the book and picture
Flesh felt or paper for hands
Thin balsa wood
½ yd. 1 inch deep gathered lace frilling
Narrow lace for pillow and sheet

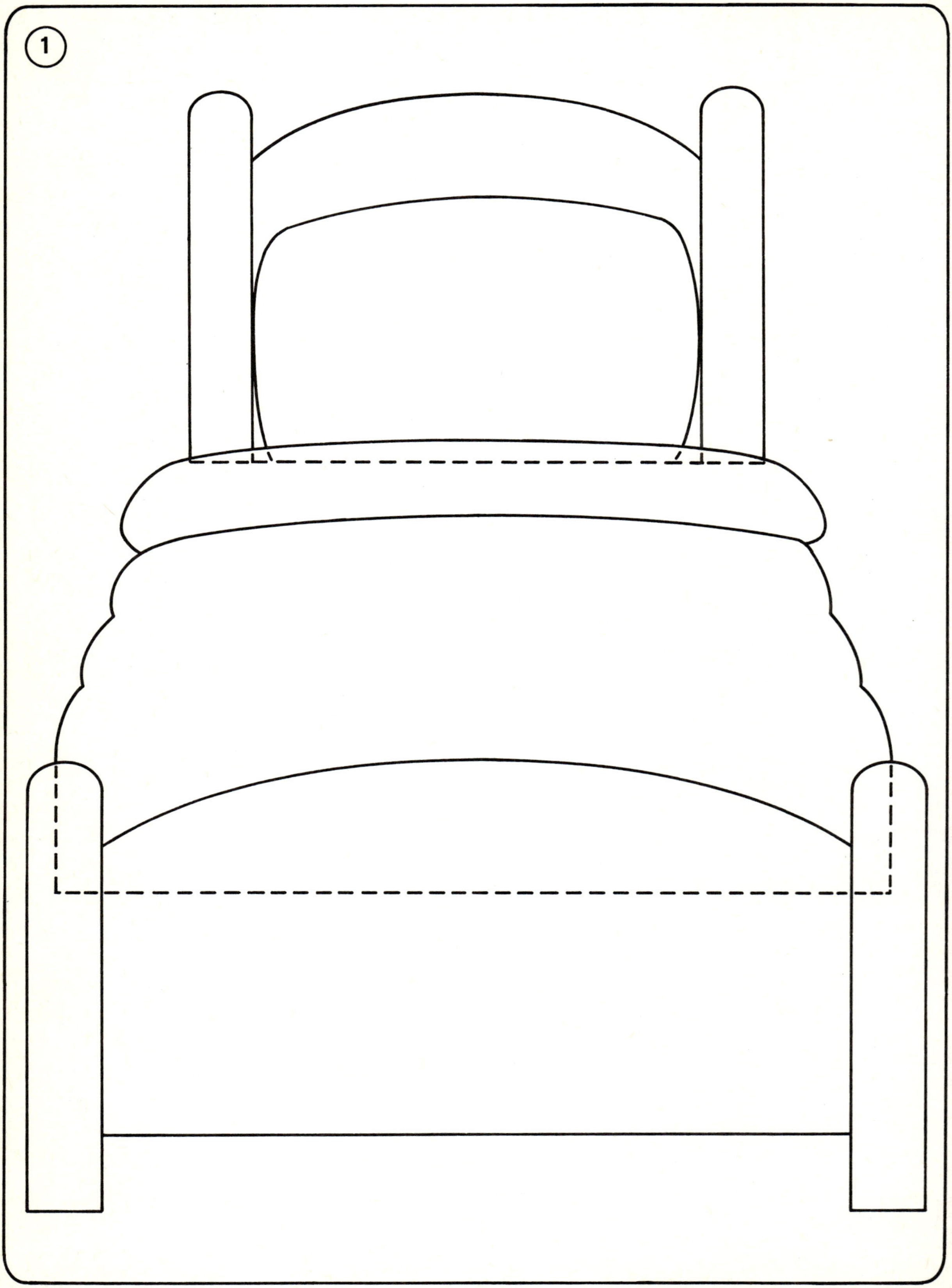
1

Materials: (cont.)

Narrow braids for picture frame and tablecloth
Fringe for the rug
3-ply or 4-ply brown knitting wool for hair
Flat round button – about $\frac{3}{4}$ inch diameter for vase
Tiny gilt beads for drawer handles
Tiny artificial flowers
Fine chain to hang picture
Round wooden lolly stick for curtain rail
Wooden cocktail sticks for stool
Gift-wrap paper motifs – or alternative
14 inch square cake stand, or stiff card
$1\frac{3}{4}$ yards decorative braid to frame
Double-sided tape (optional)
Wallpaper paste
Do-it-yourself fabric adhesive
Clear all-purpose adhesive

Method: Trace the outline of the *whole* bed (diagram 1) on to white cartridge paper. Then trace the foot of the bed only, on to a second piece of paper, and cut both shapes out.

Cut a piece of thin balsa wood 3 inches long by at least $2\frac{1}{2}$ inches deep. Stick to the paper bed-head between the two side posts and level with the broken line: then carefully trim the top round with a sharp craft knife, level with the curve of the paper. Cut two strips at least $2\frac{1}{2}$ inches long for the posts, the same width as diagram 1, and stick at each side of the central piece, level with the broken line: carve the rounded tops level with the paper, as before.

Cut another piece of balsa 5 inches long by at least $2\frac{1}{2}$ inches deep, and stick to the *separate* foot of the bed, curving the top as for the head. Then cut two $\frac{1}{2}$ inch wide strips at least 3 inches long, and use for the posts at each side, finishing the tops as previously.

Trace the pillow (to the broken line) on to Vilene and cut out. Cover with suitable fabric – I used a softly-printed flowered cotton – then stick narrow lace to the back to overlap the top and side edges. Stick into position on the bed-head.

Trace the sheet on to Vilene, then cover with the same fabric and edge with lace as illustrated.

Trace the coverlet on to Vilene, the top and bottom edges level with the broken lines. Cover with fabric – I used a patterned dress cotton – then stick to the paper bed. Stick the sheet on top of the coverlet. Now stick the separate foot of the bed into position.

I cut motifs from gift-wrap paper to decorate the foot of the bed (see picture).

Trace the child in diagram 2 on to Vilene and cut out. Stick strands of wool closely side-by-side to cover the head (I used double-sided tape) overlapping the rounded top and the edge of the book, as for the Red Indians in chapter 3. Stick the surplus at the top neatly over to the back, as in the previous instance.

Trace the book on to coloured paper and cut out. Stick to the Vilene, covering the ends of the wool. Rule a line down the centre in black ink, and write the title on the cover.

Cut the hands in flesh-coloured felt or paper, and stick one at each side, over the edges of the book.

Stick the figure to the bed, positioning as illustrated.

Cut a piece of white cartridge paper $4\frac{1}{2}$ inches wide by $3\frac{1}{2}$ inches deep, for the window (see diagram 3). Stick a $3\frac{1}{2}$ inch square of mid-blue paper

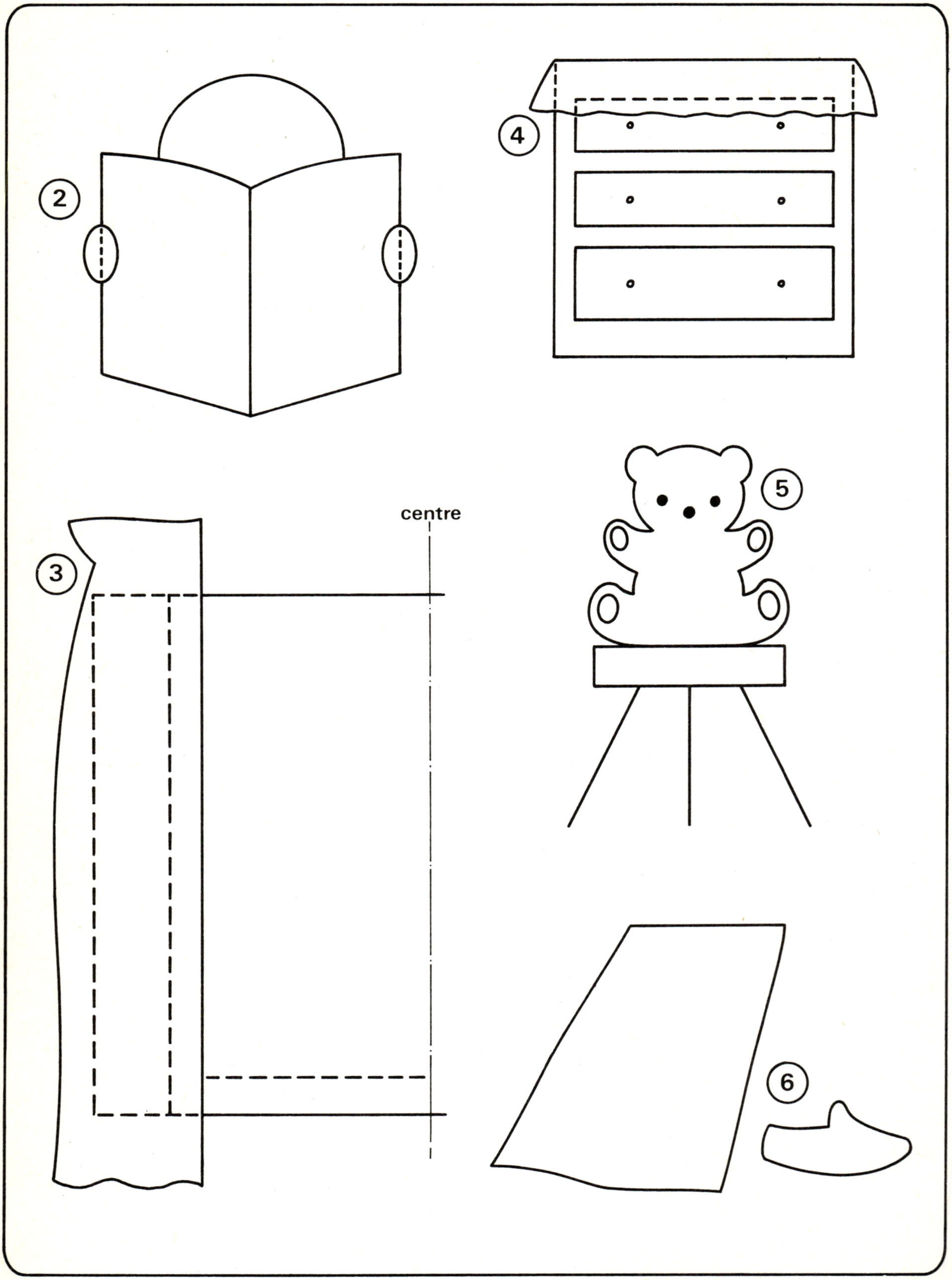
2
4
5
centre
3
6

to the white, level with the top and bottom edges, but with $\frac{1}{2}$ inch overlapping equally at each side. Cut a 3 inch long strip of balsa $\frac{1}{4}$ inch wide, and stick centrally over the blue along the lower edge, for the sill.

Beginning with the lowest row, stick layers of gathered lace all the way up the window as illustrated, the bottom edge of each upper row just overlapping the top of the one below.

Trace the curtain (diagram 3) on to Vilene twice, reversing the pattern for the second one. Cut out and cover with fabric. Then stick at each side of the window, as indicated in diagram 3, over the cut ends of the lace, and overlapping above, below and at each side.

Cut a 2 inch square of balsa wood for the chest. Then cut three pieces for the drawers (in even thinner balsa, if possible) following the measurements in diagram 4. Stick to the front of the chest. Then stick a pair of tiny gilt beads to each drawer for handles, as indicated.

Trace the cloth on to Vilene and cover with fabric – leaving $\frac{1}{2}$ inch overlapping at the top edge. Trim the lower edge with braid or lace, then stick over upper part of chest as indicated. Fold the surplus fabric at the top over to the back and stick down neatly.

Cut a suitable subject for the picture from gift-wrap paper or alternative, and make into a picture roughly $2\frac{1}{4}$ inches deep by $1\frac{3}{4}$ inches wide, following the illustration. I framed mine with narrow braid, and fixed a $2\frac{1}{2}$ inch length of fine chain to the top corners.

Trace a pattern for the bear from diagram 5, and cut in gold felt. Cut circles (I used different sizes on a leather-punch) in black and brown for the features and paws, and stick into position.

Cut a $\frac{1}{4}$ inch wide strip of balsa $1\frac{1}{4}$ inches long for the top of the stool, and three pieces of cocktail stick to the measurements in diagram 5, for the legs.

Trace a pattern for the rug from diagram 6, and cut in a rough textured fabric – I used towelling. Stick fringe to the back at each short end, and trim to length (shorter at the back).

Trace the slipper from diagram 6 and cut twice in felt, reversing the pattern for the second one.

Paste paper or alternative wall covering $9\frac{1}{2}$ inches deep to cover the upper section of the cake stand or card. Then cut felt or alternative floor covering 5 inches deep, and stick to the lower section of the board, covering the lower edge of the walls.

When quite dry, arrange and re-arrange all the items in position following my version from the illustration, or making your own arrangement, just as you prefer.

When you are quite satisfied, mark the position of each item with pins, and then stick into place, beginning with the bed.

Then stick the window into position, leaving the top of each curtain unstuck. Stick a round wooden lolly stick above the window for the curtain rail, as illustrated, and then stick the tops of the curtains down over it.

Stick the chest down, then stick the button with the edge against the top of the cloth, and stick flowers and leaves around and above.

Stick the bear into position, then stick the seat of the stool beneath him, followed by the cocktail stick legs, following diagram 5.

Stick the rug and picture to the floor and wall respectively, fixing a bead above the picture from which to hang the chain. I drove a tiny pin through the bead and chain and into the cake stand for this. Stick the slippers at different angles, as illustrated.

Stick decorative braid all round the edge to frame. I chose one woven in colours which picked up those of the picture.

5 Drawing from nature

Natural materials combine to form very different types of collage for these two examples of a quite new aspect of the craft. Colourful dried everlasting flowers and foliage form a delicate arrangement in a wooden frame – contrasted against a bold, stylised flower design, made up of dried pulse vegetables, straight from the larder!

Although I haven't done so, it can be fun to make this even more a store-cupboard composition by incorporating various forms of pasta as well: spaghetti, macaroni, vermicelli, noodles, etcetera, are available in an exciting range of shapes – straight, curled, squares, rings and shells – and it's tempting to include some of these, too. However, I have restricted **my** interpretation to split peas, butter beans, lentils, pearl barley and rice – drawn together with white cord. But you will probably have very different ideas on the subject.

Summer Garden

Illustrated in colour on page 25

Straw-daisies and statice combine with oats and grasses – some dyed, some bleached – for this evocative composition set in a rustic frame. This type of picture is always popular, and makes a delightful and impressive gift.

You will be surprised how very few flower-heads and pieces of foliage you need to make an effective picture. If you buy a few bunches at a time, you will soon find you have a good collection from which to select materials for a never-ending series of flower collages similar to this one. It is also often possible to obtain special colour-schemed packs of assorted materials, and these supply ideal material for this type of collage.

And you might be interested to learn the secret of my rich, creamy woven background, which is a perfect foil for the arrangement. Although it **looks** like an expensive linen, it is in fact the special lining canvas sold for making men's ties!

Materials:

Dried everlasting flowers and foliage – dyed and/or bleached: I used straw-daisies (helichrysums), statice, oats and various grasses
Natural fabric for the background (see above)
8 inch square cake stand – or stiff card 8 ins. by 6 ins.
Strip of $\frac{1}{4}$ inch thick balsa, or other wood, 9 inches long by 3 inches wide (or two pieces this size for a deeper frame)
Tiny pins
Clear all-purpose adhesive

Method: Cut your cake stand or card to size – 8 inches by 6 inches – with a sharp knife. Cover completely – sides as well – with background

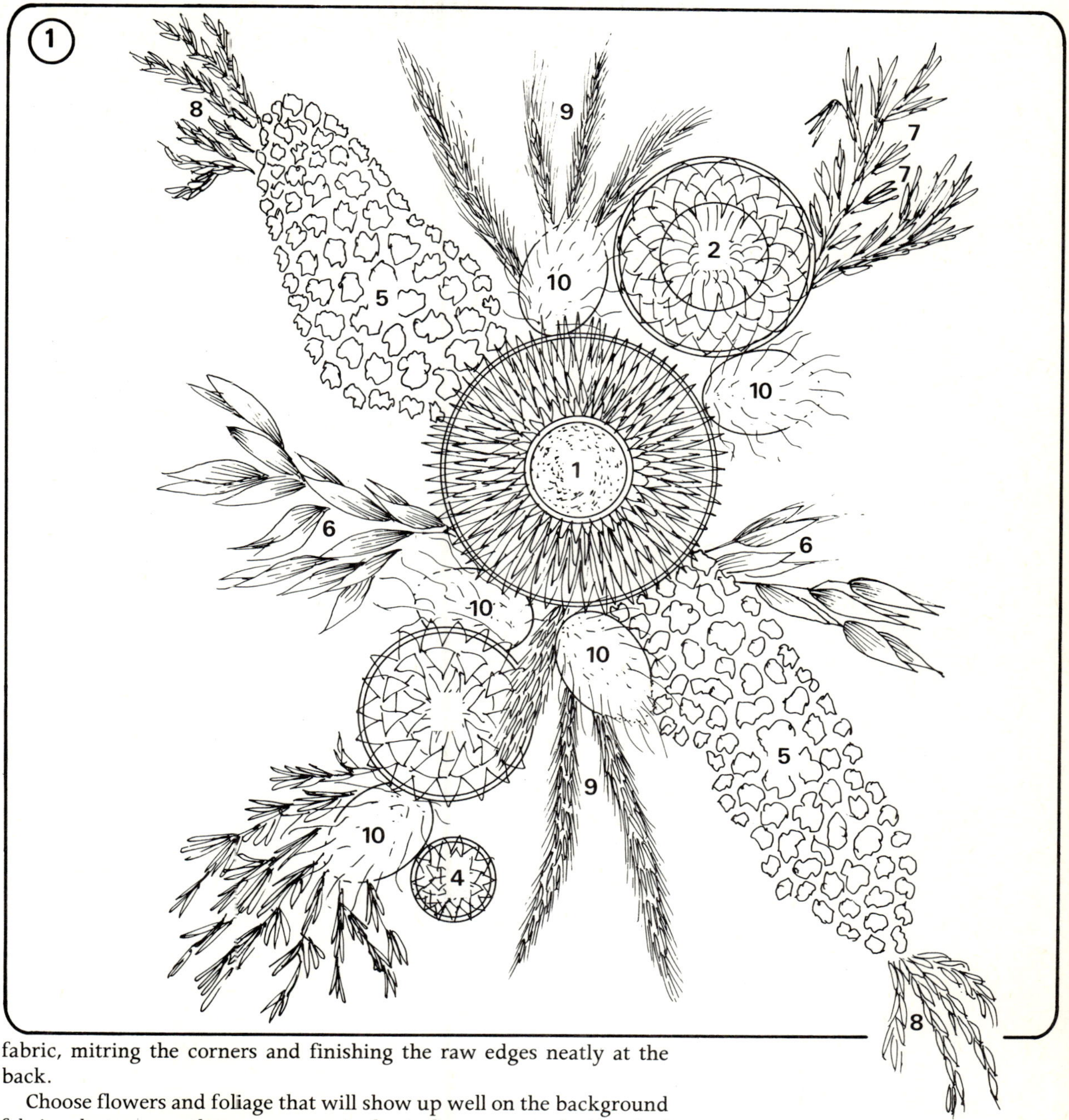

fabric, mitring the corners and finishing the raw edges neatly at the back.

Choose flowers and foliage that will show up well on the background fabric – but arrange them on a separate sheet of paper cut to the identical size. Trim away any stalk or other protuberance at the back of the straw-daisies (or other flat flowers you are using) and place them in a central arrangement radiating diagonally towards the corners, as illustrated. Add tiny pieces of statice, or other flowers, to build up spikes in the direction of the other corners. Then add tiny heads of grass and oats to extend and fill in the design, as shown. I have sketched out my arrangement, numbering the pieces to indicate the order in which I worked. You will find that nature tends to take over and do much of the designing for you, as the pieces fall naturally into place as you move them about.

When you are satisfied with your arrangement, mount each piece down separately, beginning at the centre, and working in much the same order as you originally composed the design (see diagram). Use clear all-purpose adhesive – generously coating the backs of the larger pieces, and adding tiny pins, the heads concealed in the petals, to hold securely in place if necessary. Always rest the piece in position on the background before sticking it down, so that you can see exactly where to apply the adhesive – then press down into place. Tuck the tiny stalks of the grass-heads and oats behind the larger pieces, and fill in the centre with the fluffier pieces. A thin trail of adhesive along the back of the grasses will hold them securely: always begin at the base and work towards the tip.

To make the frame, cut the wood into four equal $\frac{3}{4}$ inch wide, 9 inch long strips (or $1\frac{1}{2}$ inch wide strips for a deeper frame). Cut two of these strips $7\frac{1}{2}$ inches long, and the other two 8 inches long. From the remaining ends, cut four pieces $\frac{1}{2}$ inch long.

Stick and pin the two longer pieces at the sides of your picture, overlapping the front and level with the top and bottom corners. Then stick and pin the two shorter pieces across the top and bottom, overlapping equally at each end. Finally, stick the four short pieces at right-angles to the top and bottom of the frame, to extend the sides as illustrated.

Flowers in the Sun

Illustrated in colour on page 28

The secret of this collage technique lies in the adhesive: lots and lots of it! Do be really generous in applying it, as some will soak into the background, and plenty is needed to hold the pulses (or pasta) firmly in position and prevent them dropping off – especially when you sprinkle barley or rice to fill in large areas.

The linking stems could be different thicknesses of ordinary household string, though I prefer to use varying weights of piping cord.

Materials: Dried pulse vegetables (and pasta, if liked): I used butter beans, green split peas, yellow split peas, lentils, pearl barley and rice
Thick, and thinner, white parcel string, or fine and medium-weight piping cords (Numbers 1 and 3)
Hessian or similar woven fabric for the background
14 inch diameter circular cake stand, or stiff card
Do-it-yourself fabric adhesive
Clear all-purpose adhesive

Method: Cover the cake stand or card with the background fabric, allowing it to overlap about 2 inches all round: snip this surplus into tabs all the way round, and stick each one neatly to the back of the board.

Trace the two circular centres and three petals in diagram 1 on to thick paper or thin card, and cut out.

Decide the positions your flowers are to occupy, then mark the outline of each one as follows. Pin the circular centre to the board (the larger circle for the largest flower – the smaller for the other two). Draw round it using a wax china-marking pencil, or a dressmaker's chalk. Mark the end of each radiating line very accurately against the outer edge of the circle. Remove the circular pattern and then place the appropriate petal against the outer edge of the circle, between a pair of marks, and draw round it. Remove the pattern and repeat four more times to complete the flower.

Decide what you are going to use to create your flower, arranging a small section on the background to see how it will look. When you are satisfied, squeeze some clear all-purpose adhesive into the centre, and arrange these pieces as illustrated. Spread more adhesive round the centre if you plan to make a larger circle (as I have done for the largest flower), and arrange these pieces. For the smallest flower, I made a neat flat coil of fine piping cord, and stuck this into place for the centre.

To make the petals, run a trail of adhesive over the marked line (do one petal at a time), and then make a neat edge all the way round, placing your chosen pieces side-by-side, making sure they are roughly the same size. Then add any centre decoration to each petal in the same way. Finally, to fill the petals with small grains, squeeze the adhesive very liberally over the whole area, then sprinkle a generous amount over it and press down firmly so that as much as possible is held. Gently shake off any surplus.

I used green split peas surrounded by two circles of lentils for my large flower: the petals are edged with yellow peas, and more green ones form the central lines – then the remainder of the petal is filled in with pearl barley.

The middle flower also has a centre of green peas – with a butter bean for each petal surrounded by rows of yellow peas.

Lentils edge the petals of the strong-centred smallest flower – filled in with rice.

Trace a pattern for the leaf from diagram 2, as for the petals, and draw round it in the same way in the positions required.

Run a very narrow trail of fabric adhesive over the outline, and then press string or fine piping cord neatly over it, with the cut ends meeting at the base. Fill in as required – in the same way as the petals: I simply made one line of green peas against the inner edge of the cord, leaving the green fabric of the background to form the centre of the leaf.

Link the design together with thicker string or piping cord, marking the position of the lines and then sticking it into place with fabric adhesive. I unravelled the cord to form three veins on each leaf, cutting them to length, as illustrated.

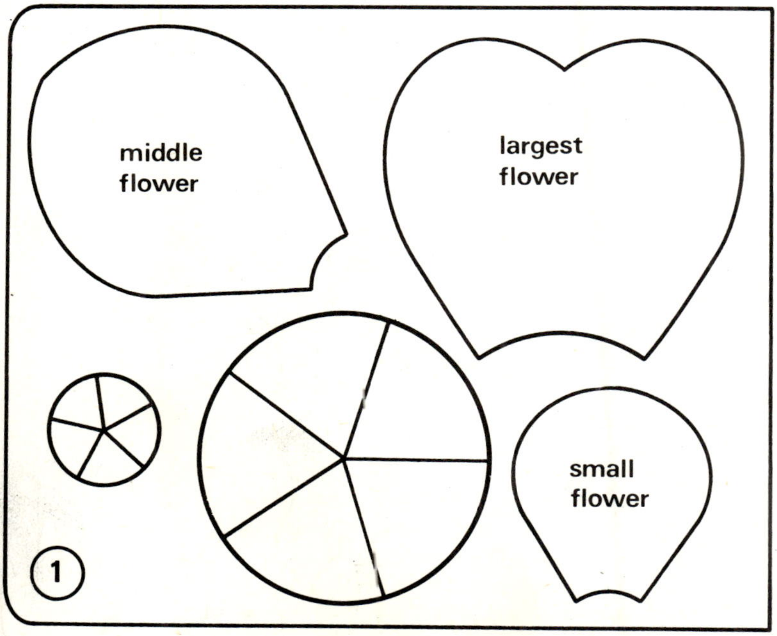

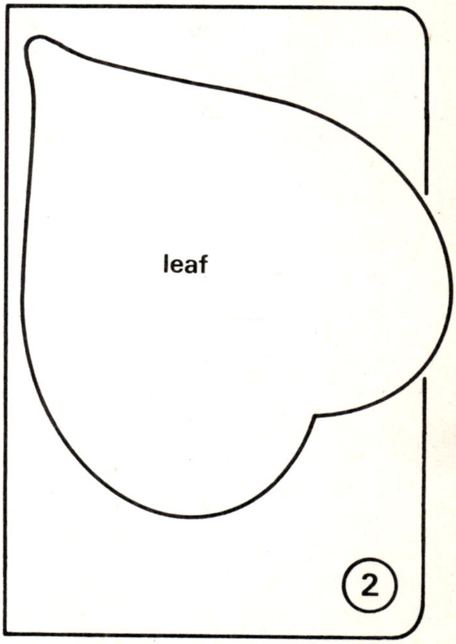

6 Flights of fancy

Ornithologists, please study elsewhere! Birds are always a popular subject for collage – but mainly because they afford so much exciting opportunity for free interpretation. And artist's license is an acceptable excuse for the most fantastic creations you like to invent.

I have again designed two completely contrasting examples – this time with only the subject in common. Each is equally striking in its own very individual way: the turtle doves created entirely in white cord (or string) – the bird of paradise as exotic as tinsel braids, sequins and feathers can make him.

Pair of Turtle Doves

Illustrated in colour on page 29

Thick white parcel string could also be used for this design: but I prefer working with piping cord – the finest weight – as it is much easier to manipulate and, I think, gives a more pleasing effect.

I have used a combination of fabric adhesive and wallpaper paste to stick the cord into place. Working with fabric adhesive **can** be a little traumatic to begin with, though you soon get used to it. However, if you prefer, you can use wallpaper paste throughout: the only advantage of fabric adhesive is that the cord is held immediately, whereas you have to wait for the paste-soaked cord to dry before it is securely stuck, so you must be careful not to dislodge previously worked pieces accidentally as you continue with the design elsewhere.

Materials:
Fine white piping cord (about 10 yards – Number 1) – or good quality heavy white household string
Hessian or similar woven fabric for background
12 inch square cake stand or stiff card
Wallpaper paste
Do-it-yourself fabric adhesive

Method: Cover the cake stand or card with background fabric, allowing it to overlap 2 inches all round: mitre the corners and stick surplus neatly round to the back of the board.

Trace the outline shape of the bird on to thin card from diagram 1: mark the position of the eye. Then trace the wing separately – and the wing again, but this time ending at the scalloped edge, above the three feathers at the tip. Cut these three pieces of card out, making a hole in the centre of the eye.

The safest way to decide the position of the two birds on your picture is to fold a piece of white paper in half, draw round your card pattern on one side and then cut the shape out in the double paper, so that you have two birds. Place these on the background, and when you are happy with their position in relation to each other, mark the tips of the beak, wing and tail of each with pins.

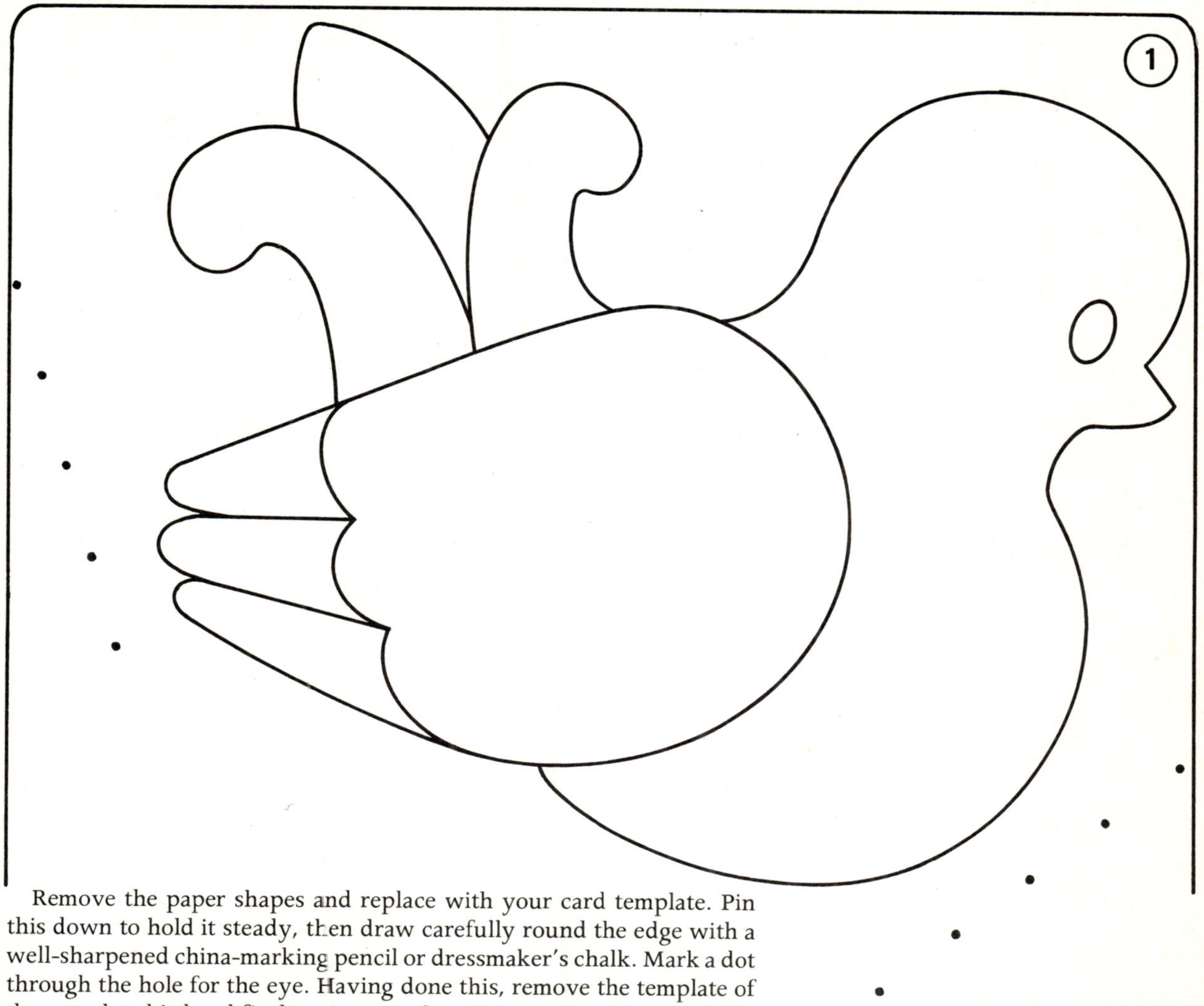

Remove the paper shapes and replace with your card template. Pin this down to hold it steady, then draw carefully round the edge with a well-sharpened china-marking pencil or dressmaker's chalk. Mark a dot through the hole for the eye. Having done this, remove the template of the complete bird and fit the wing template into position, aligned at top and bottom: draw round that part of the edge which is not already marked. Finally, fit the smaller wing template into the shape, and mark the scalloped edge. Repeat for the second bird, reversing the patterns.

Begin to work the shape of the bird in cord with the two outer, curled, tail feathers. I used fabric adhesive, applying it with the point of a very fine stick (a cocktail stick would do), running a very thin trail along the marked line. Then press the cord down into the adhesive, beginning and ending against the edge of the wing. When you have outlined the shape, fill it in with two more curled pieces of cord, as illustrated, sticking it down in exactly the same way.

Having completed both the outer tail feathers, outline the centre section, and then fill in with three more lengths of cord, following the outline.

Next work the three lower feathers of the wing in the same way, outlining each and then adding an inner length of double cord. Then make the scallops, continuing the cord to outline the whole of the upper part of the wing. Having done this, stick a wavy line of cord inside the wing, a little away from, but following the line of, the previous row of scallops: continue the cord round the upper part of the wing, but stick it right up against the inside edge of the outline. Repeat with another

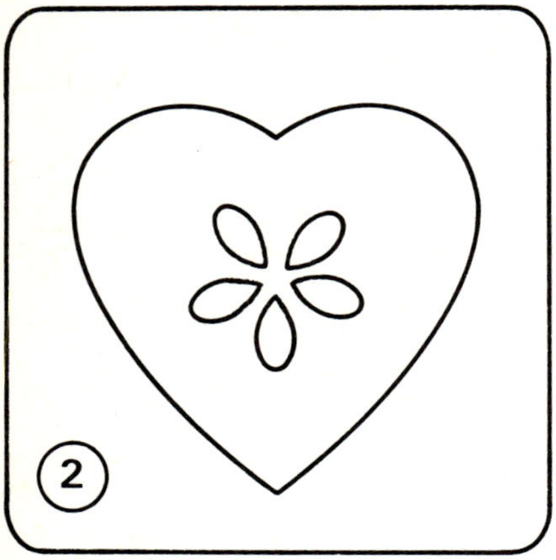

scalloped line an equal distance away from the second one, and then take the cord round the upper part of the wing, against the inner edge of the previous row, as before.

Make five inner "feathers" as follows. Cut a 1 inch length of cord: dab a spot of fabric adhesive against the two cut ends, then twist them together between the fingertips to join and form a teardrop shape. Cut a 2 inch length of cord and form into a similar shape in the same way. Then place the smaller inside the larger, and when you have made all five, arrange them in position inside the wing. When you have decided an attractive arrangement, mark each feather's position with pins and stick them into place.

Now outline the head and body of the bird, following the marked line carefully. Make four more feathers from 1 inch lengths of cord and stick to the breast, as illustrated.

To make the eye, coil a 2 inch length of cord into a slightly oval shape, then stick into position.

Complete the second bird in exactly the same way.

To make the nest, trace the five dots at each side of the bird in diagram 1 on to a piece of tissue paper. Place this flat on the fabric in position below the birds, and drive a pin through each dot so that it is securely held in the mount. Then gently tear away the tissue paper.

Now, starting against the pin at the top left corner, press the beginning of a long length of cord *absolutely saturated in wallpaper paste* down on to the fabric, taking it across and *underneath* the right hand pin, round it and back to go under and round the top pin on the left hand side. Continue in this way, taking the saturated cord across, under and round the second pin on the right hand side, then back to the second pin on the left and so on, finishing the cut end of the cord at the lowest pin on the right hand side. Adjust the cords to cross neatly, as illustrated, if necessary, and then leave to dry out thoroughly.

Trace the heart shape in diagram 2 on to thin card, cut out and mark the outline on the fabric above the birds as before, following the illustration. Outline with cord in the usual way, then make a flower from five $\frac{3}{4}$ inch lengths of cord made into teardrop shapes as for the feathers, and stick in the centre.

Bird of Paradise

Illustrated in colour on page 49

The choice of materials for this design is very much your own. You might even decide on glistening foil papers instead of fabrics or braids – with perhaps the tall feathers cut in tissue paper only lightly held in position with adhesive. I used glittering tinsel braid in vivid colours (incidentally, your colouring will probably be quite different from mine, which is only intended as a guide – depending far more on what one has available than the picture in the reference book): I stole my feathers from a pair of gay feather dusters, and added more sparkle with shining sequins.

Such extravagant materials and colourings need an absolutely plain, dull background. I found cheap black calico proved the perfect foil for my exotic bird.

Materials: Medium-weight Vilene or Pellon
Rich fabrics, foil papers or tinsel braids for the head and body: I used narrow tinsel braid in pink, deep red, green, blue and gold

Materials: (cont.)

Feathers: I used yellow and orange
1 inch diameter gold sequin (optional) for beak – or gold foil paper
Sequins, bead, etcetera, for eye (see below)
Strings of sequins for the plumes: I used purple and lilac
Sequins or alternative for feet (see below)
$\frac{1}{4}$ yard $\frac{1}{2}$ inch wide brown silk braid for branch
14 inch square cake stand, or stiff card 14 inches by $9\frac{1}{2}$ inches
Fabric for background: I used black calico
$1\frac{1}{2}$ yards gilt braid to frame
Wallpaper paste
Do-it-yourself fabric adhesive
Clear all-purpose adhesive

Method: Trace the bird in diagram 1 on to Vilene and cut out.

Begin with the tail. Arrange yellow feathers on the Vilene, the upper ones overlapping the tops of those beneath, and the top feathers overlapping the edge of the body. When the Vilene is sufficiently covered, and you are happy with the arrangement, *stick the tops only* to the Vilene. Insert a few orange feathers between the yellow ones, as illustrated, and when you are satisfied with this, stick the tops of those into place as before, hidden under the yellow feathers.

If using fabric or paper, trace patterns for the various shapes, cut out and stick down as in previous collages. If using narrow tinsel braid as I have done, stick a row of pink round the top of the head, level with the edge of the Vilene, and following the direction of the arrows. Follow with a second line of braid running parallel to the first, and right up against it, so that no gap is visible. Continue until the section is filled, according to the width of your braid (mine took three rows).

Stick a short length of blue between the eye and neck, as illustrated. Then fill in section 3 with green braid, again following the direction of the arrows.

Now work the body, section 4, in red, beginning at the top, against the wing, and following the arrows round (the edge of the braid level with the edge of the Vilene) to the tip of the wing. Stick parallel rows of braid to fill in the entire body section as before.

Make the wing from gold braid, beginning at the lower tip, and following the arrows all the way round the edge to finish over the previous cut end at the lower tip. Stick similar rows of braid inside each previous row until the wing is completely covered.

I cut the shape of the beak from a large gold sequin, sticking it to the Vilene with clear all-purpose adhesive – but gold foil paper would do as well.

The eye could be made up in all manner of ways. I used a fluted silver sequin with a black sequin and a small black glass-headed pin in the centre (so I didn't, in fact, add it until I had mounted the bird down). But a sparkling diamanté "jewel" from a broken brooch set on a dark sequin – a black bead circled with tiny glass ones, or seed pearls – a glittering button . . . the possibilities are endless, and rely on your own initiative and imagination.

Cut your cake stand or card to size – 14 inches by $9\frac{1}{2}$ inches.

Cover it with your background fabric, cutting the fabric 2 inches larger all round, pasting it to the front of the mount, then mitring the corners and sticking the surplus neatly round to the back.

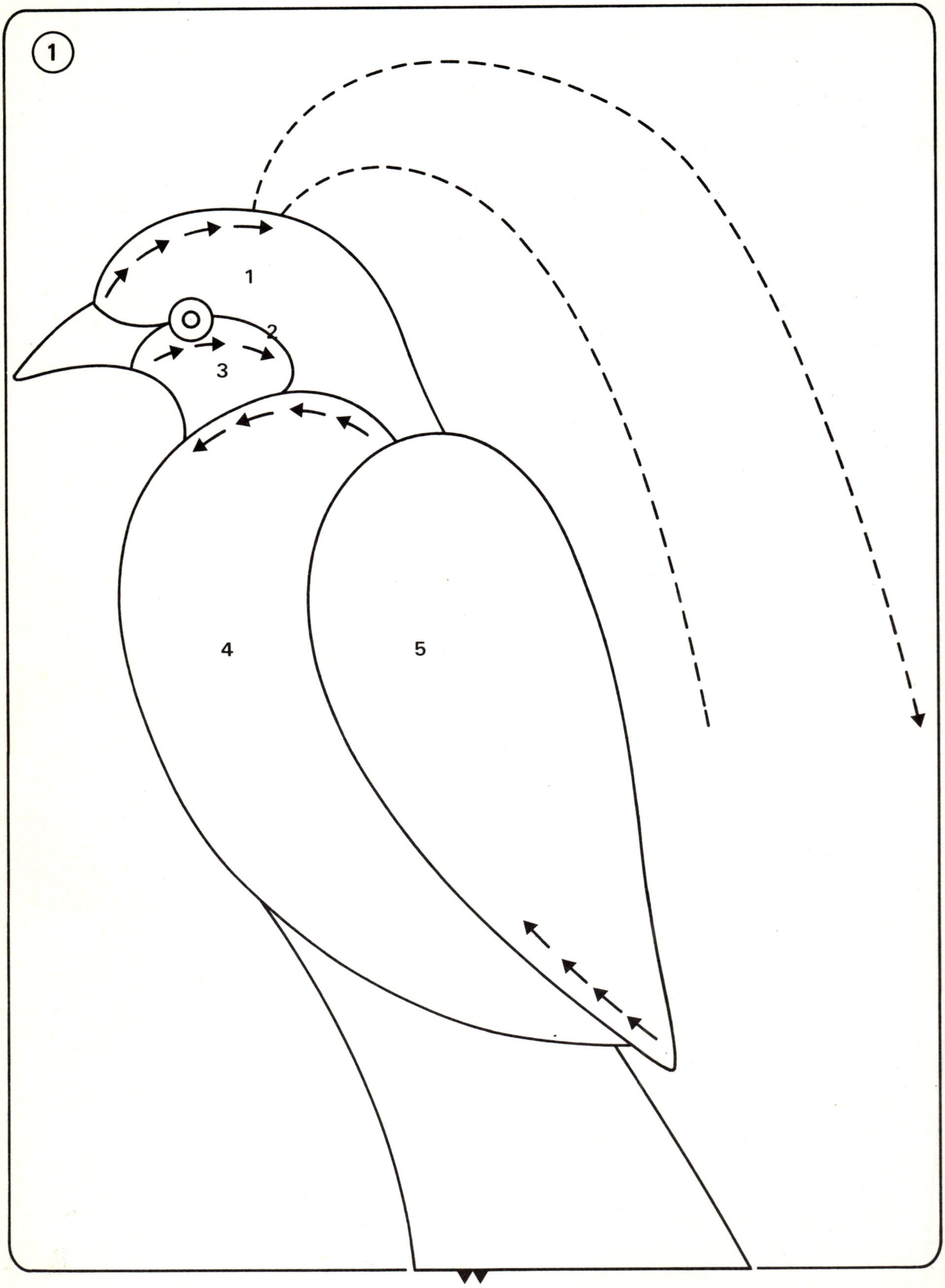
1
1
2
3
4
5

Place the bird on the mount to determine its position, then mark with pins before removing the collage and covering the back of the Vilene with adhesive, *leaving about 1 inch at the bottom of the tail free.* Mount the bird down, then carefully trim away the loose Vilene at the end of the tail if you feel it is necessary: otherwise stick it lightly down.

Position the braid across the bird to form its perch, then mark with pins and stick into place.

I stuck two gold domed sequins to the branch for each foot, but plain sequins, beads or braid would all be good alternatives.

Finally, arrange strings of sequins to form two "plumes" (I used purple for the outer one and lilac for the inner), mark their positions and then stick neatly into place along a trail of adhesive (as for the turtle doves).

Stick gilt braid all round the edge to frame.

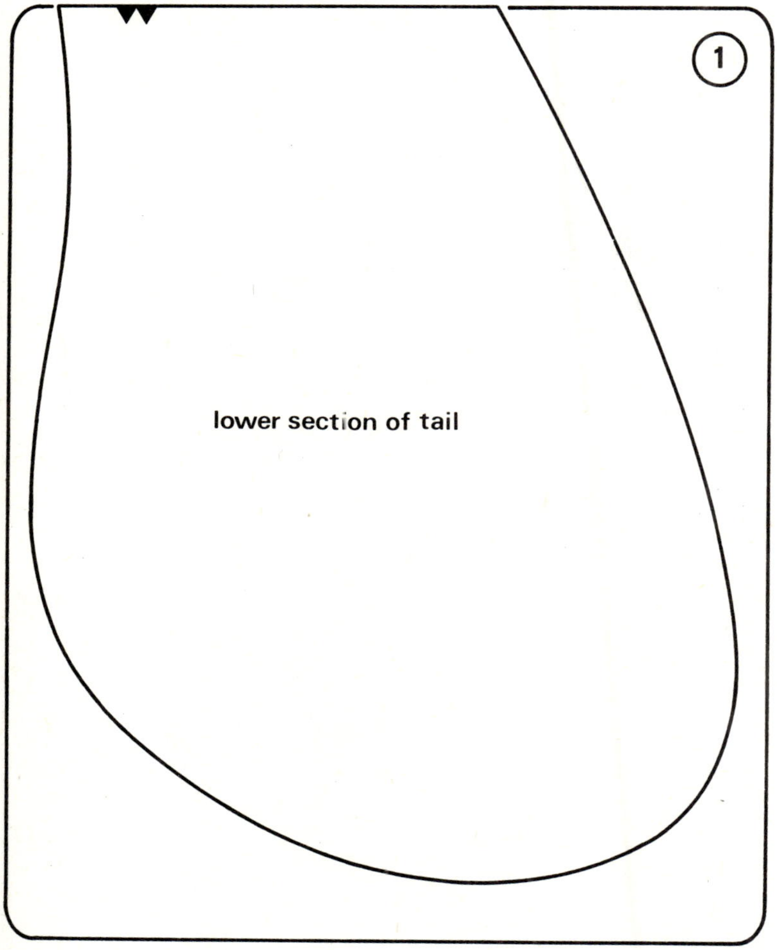

7 Sophisticated simplicity

Again two completely different collages – each illustrating how simplicity of design can create a highly sophisticated effect. The first I have called "Snowscape", and although there is a diagram to show the exact proportions of my design – so that you can follow them if you wish – you will probably enjoy sketching out your own special landscape: since, as you can see, it's only a series of curved lines of no great artistic merit! The collage relies for its impact on a careful choice of smoothly textured fabrics in contrasting, yet toning, shades. The starkness of the snowy wastes is broken by the bare branches of the bush and the tree.

The second example too, relies on subtle colour matching and texture. The daisies, in various weights, types and shades of paper, stand out three-dimensionally above their perfectly plain "alabaster" vase against a dead black background, only relieved by a few sprays of dried grass.

The secret of both designs – and of this chapter – is to resist the temptation to add any further embellishment. Once you have completed what you set out to do – stop: it's finished!

Snowscape

Although I have interpreted my landscape as a snowy scene, there's no reason why a similar design shouldn't be worked in fabrics (or papers) which give an impression of grass, grain, earth and so on (as in "The Houses on the Hill" – chapter 4). Rough, woven fabrics, tweed,

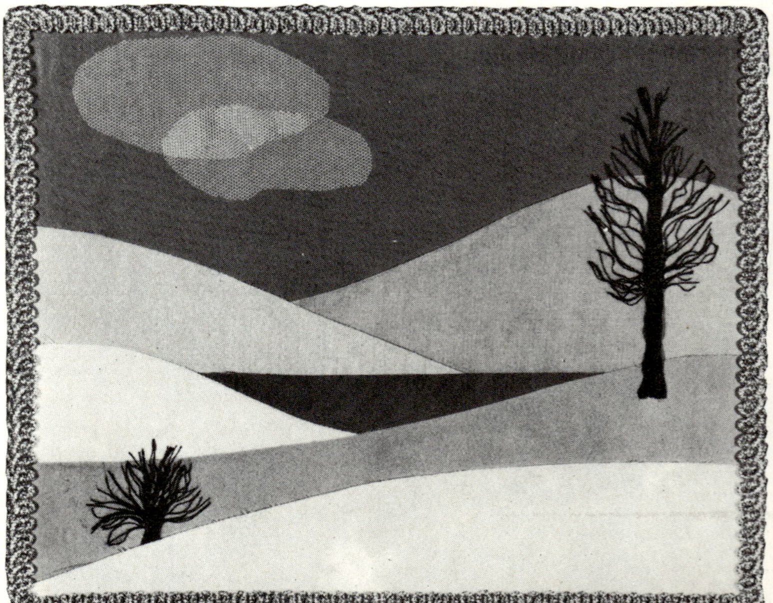

(Right) Snowscape
(Opposite) Bird of Paradise

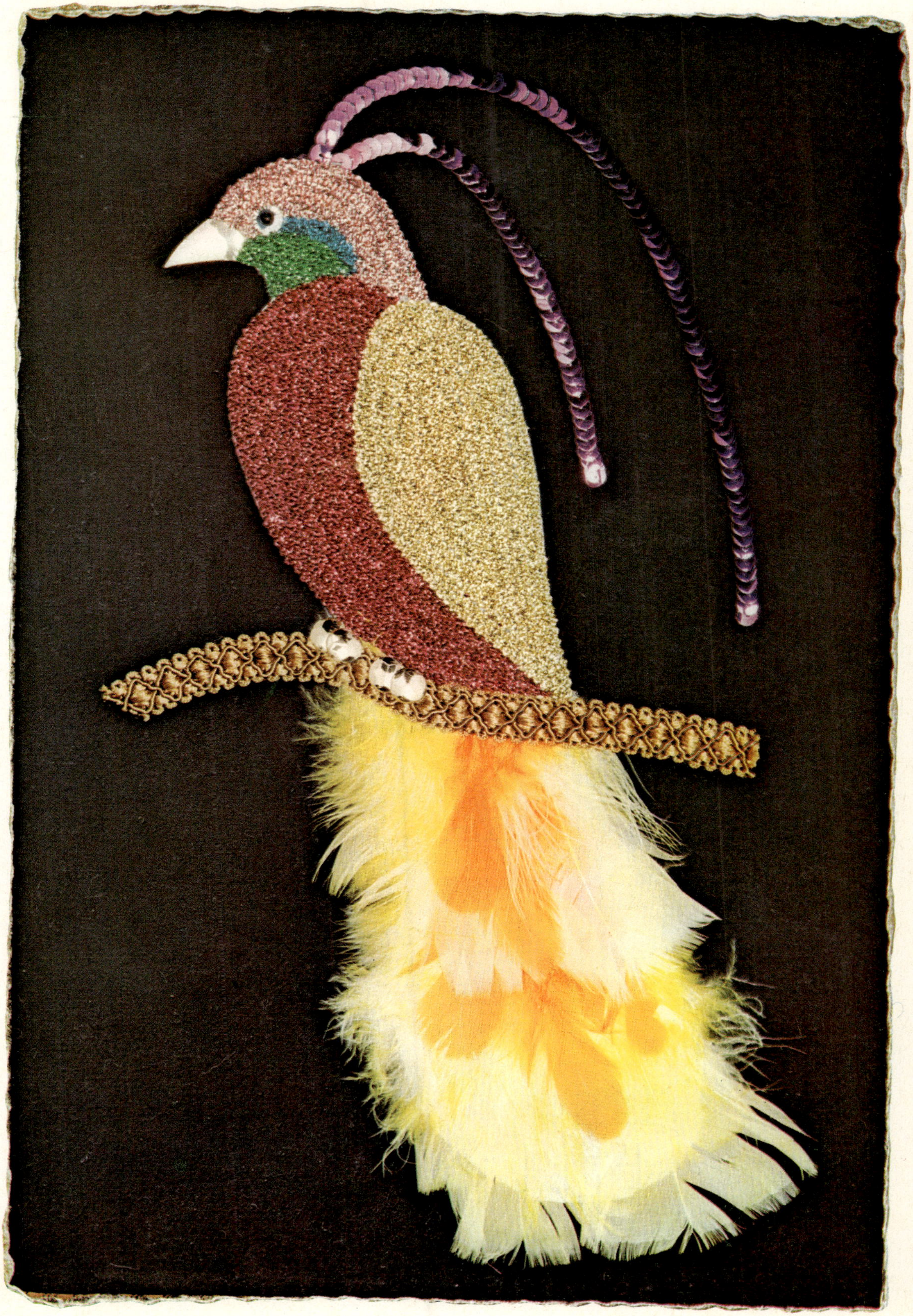

1

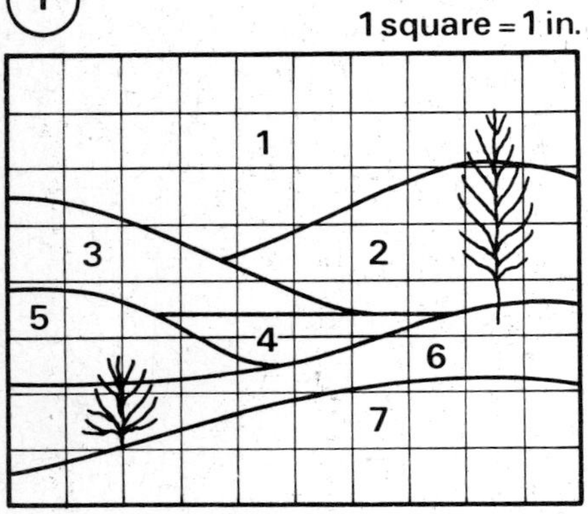

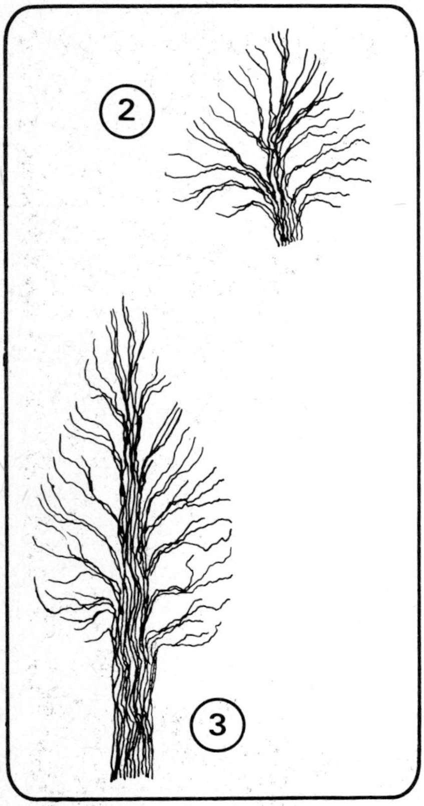

corduroy, etcetera, in varying shades of green, brown and gold create an effective landscape, carefully combined. Dull brown corduroy, for instance, makes a most convincing ploughed field. On the other hand, to achieve the glistening effect of snow and ice, I have used thin silky fabrics in softly muted shades.

When using fabric for this type of collage, I find it easiest to use an iron-on Vilene or Pellon backing. This is quite thin, and as my choice of fabrics were all rather light-weight, the pieces were not always sufficiently opaque to prevent the colour underneath showing through. So I pasted pieces of the usual medium-weight Vilene behind the ironed-on backing: however, this is only necessary when using fine fabrics.

Materials:
Iron-on Vilene or Pellon
Medium-weight Vilene or Pellon (optional – see above)
Suitable fabrics (see above – and below)
Dark brown stranded embroidery cotton
10 inch square cake stand, or stiff card 10 inches by 8 inches
1 yd. braid to frame
Wallpaper paste
Do-it-yourself fabric adhesive

Method: Either sketch out a landscape similar to mine – or rule a sheet of paper into one-inch squares and draw a pattern following diagram 1.

With the shiny (adhesive) side uppermost, trace the entire picture – excluding the tree and bush – on to the iron-on Vilene. Then cut into sections along the curved lines, so that each piece is separate.

Decide the fabrics you are going to use for each section, bearing in mind the relation of each piece to its neighbours. As a guide, you might like to know that I used blue satin for the sky, lilac silk for the right-hand mountain, with a slightly paler shade of lilac shantung for the left-hand mountain: the lake is turquoise taffeta, the bank of snow at the left and the white foreground, shantung, with the reverse (wrong) matt side of the same blue satin as the sky in between.

Carefully iron the cut-out pieces of Vilene on to the back of the appropriate fabrics, following the instructions. When cool, cut each piece out, about $\frac{1}{2}$ inch away from the Vilene – *except* along the upper edges of the mountains, the lake and the snowdrifts: cut these absolutely level with the edge of the Vilene.

If you find your pieces are not sufficiently opaque, trace the design again on to medium-weight Vilene, cut into sections as before, and paste to the backs of the various pieces to prevent the colour underneath showing through.

Cut your cake stand, or stiff card, to measure 10 inches by 8 inches.

Paste the sky into position on the mount, so that the Vilene backing is level with the top and side edges, the surplus fabric overlapping. Now paste the right-hand mountain into place, overlapping the surplus fabric along the lower edge of the sky. You will be able to see the edge of the Vilene backing the sky, and the top edge of the mountain must fit against this exactly. Follow with the left-hand mountain in the same way, then the lake, then the left-hand white snowdrift, the blue strip of shadowed snow and finally the white foreground – overlapping the side and lower edges as the sky did.

Stick the overlapping fabric neatly to the sides or back of the mount.

Cut two shapes in white net (or chiffon) for clouds and paste, one slightly overlapping the other, to the sky.

To make the bush, cut about ten $1\frac{1}{2}$ inch lengths of stranded embroidery cotton: bunch them neatly together and saturate in wallpaper paste. Then place the base against the edge of the foreground drift, as indicated in diagram 1, and gently spread out the strands, as shown in diagram 2, using a pin, and adding more paste as necessary with a fine watercolour paintbrush.

Cut about twelve $4\frac{1}{2}$ inch lengths of embroidery cotton for the tree, and work this in the same way, but begin with only two pieces of the cotton and add the remainder – well soaked in paste – one at a time, cutting each one a little shorter as you work down from the upper branches (see detail in diagram 3). Finally, add more, shorter, lengths of cotton for the lower branches, not taking them right down to the base of the trunk as for the upper ones.

When the paste is thoroughly dried out, stick braid round the edge to frame, as shown.

Daisies

Illustrated in colour on page 52

I chose a subtle colour scheme for this study in shades of brown and white on black. You may prefer to turn my daisies into asters, interpreting them in delicate pinks and mauves with yellow centres. Or, returning to the daisies, they could be in fresh, springlike green and white, again with yellow centres.

My own choice was a dull donkey brown cartridge paper behind, a thinner buff paper in between (I found the *inside* of manilla envelopes perfect for this), with white crêpe forming the delicate petals on top. The centres are crumpled brown tissue.

For the vase, I wanted a plain, heavily textured paper in a neutral, alabaster, colour. I looked through an old wallpaper sample book, certain I would have no difficulty in finding what I wanted. But every sheet was covered in violently coloured bold pattern. . . . Then suddenly I noticed that the plain *back* of every page was exactly what I was looking for – I had only to choose the most suitable texture!

Materials:

- Donkey-brown cartridge paper
- Medium-weight buff paper (see above)
- White crêpe paper
- Brown tissue paper
- Off-white or cream heavily textured paper (see above)
- Black cartridge paper for background
- Dried bleached grasses (or alternative, i.e. oats, etcetera)
- 14 inch square cake stand or stiff card
- $1\frac{1}{2}$ yards heavy cream lace or braid to frame
- Wallpaper paste
- Do-it-yourself fabric adhesive
- Clear all-purpose adhesive

Method: Make ten daisies, each one as follows. Trace the outline shape in diagram 1 on to thin card, and cut out.

Using the card as a pattern, draw round it and cut a daisy in brown paper. Now carefully fold it, right side inside, across the centre to the tips of the petals – as indicated by the broken lines. Crease well, then open out and re-fold at right-angles, repeating twice more, following the broken lines, so that there is a crease down the centre of each petal.

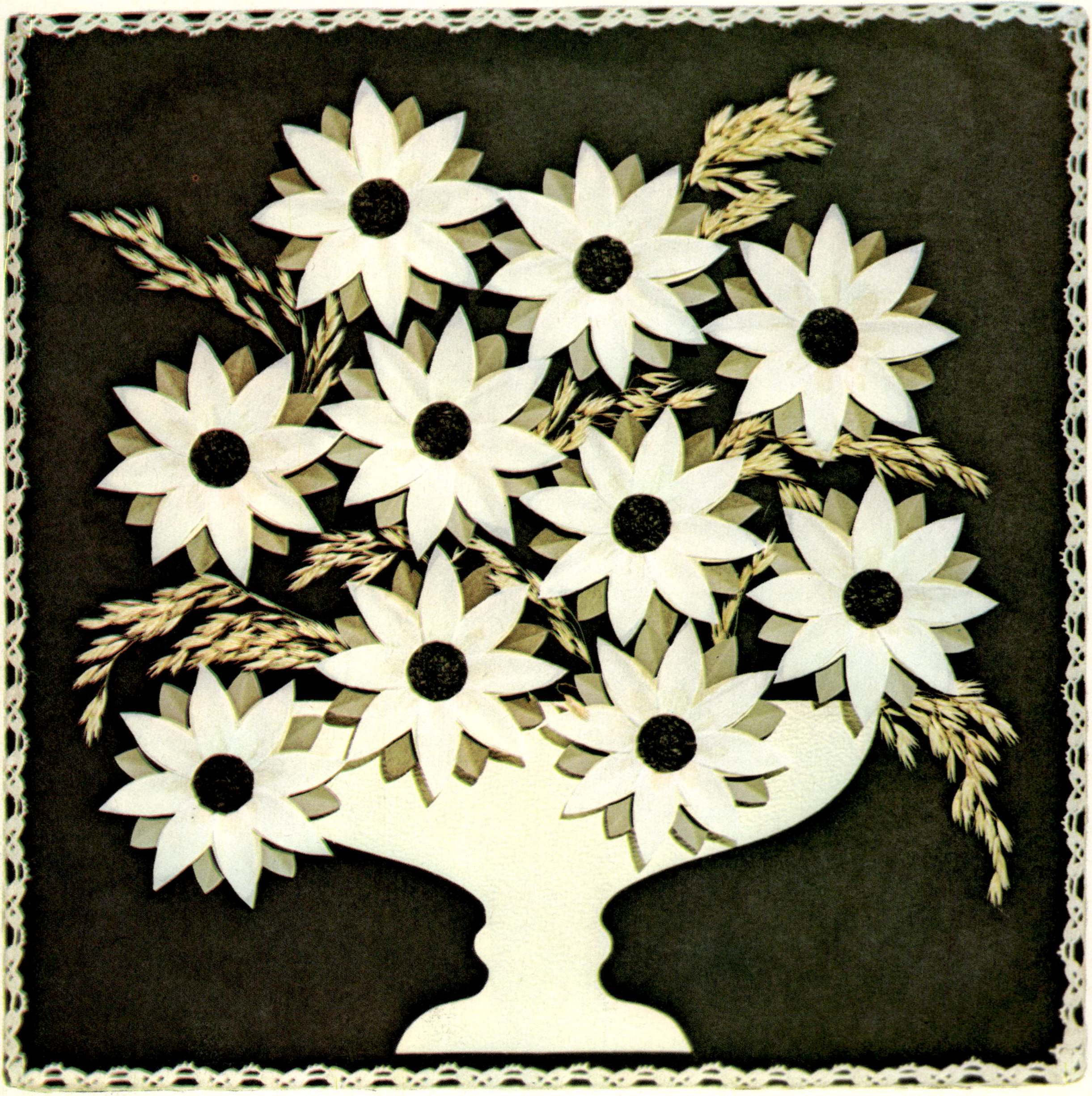

Daisies

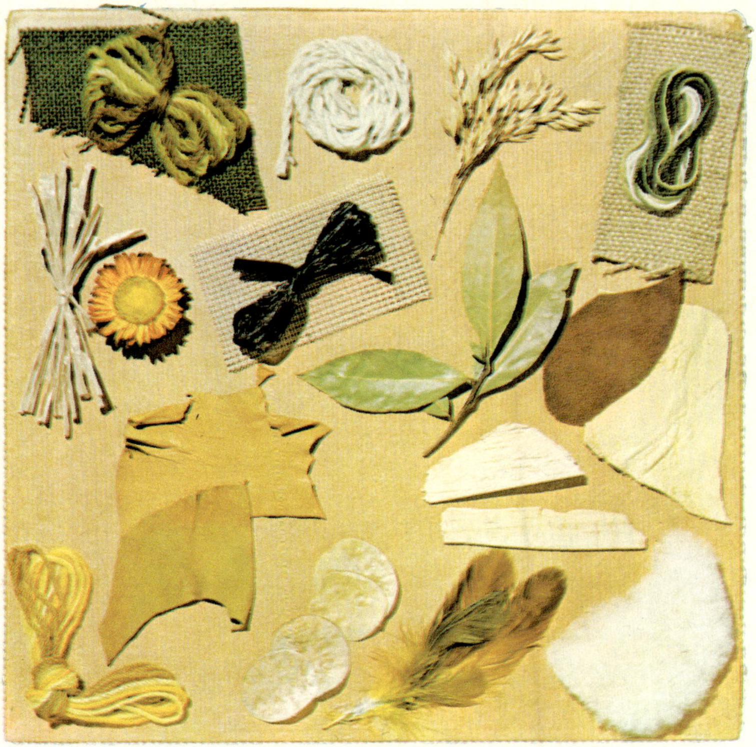

(Left) Country Memories
(Below) The Ocean Bed

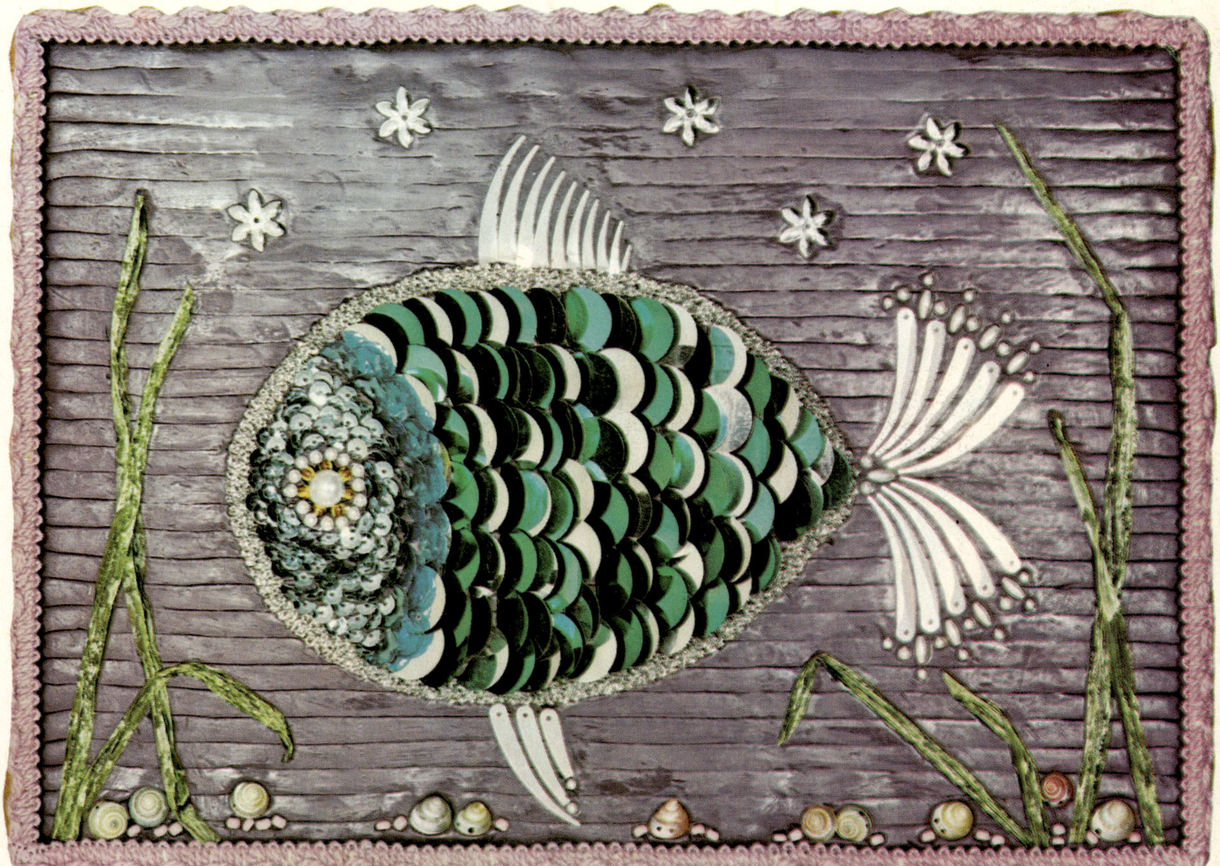

1

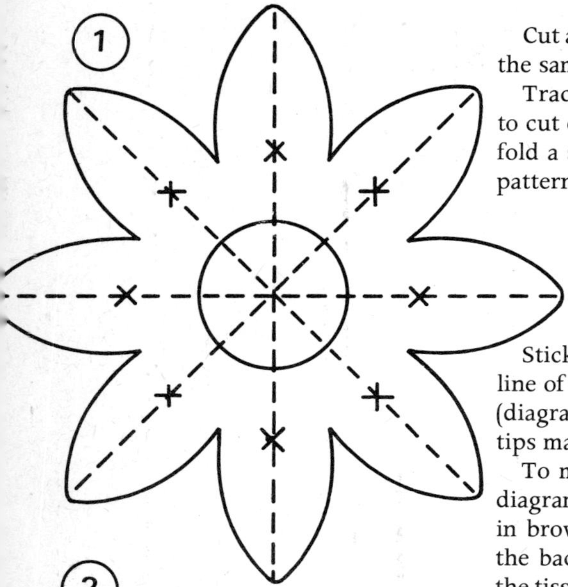

2

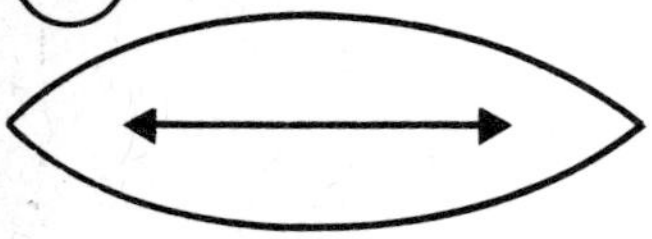

3

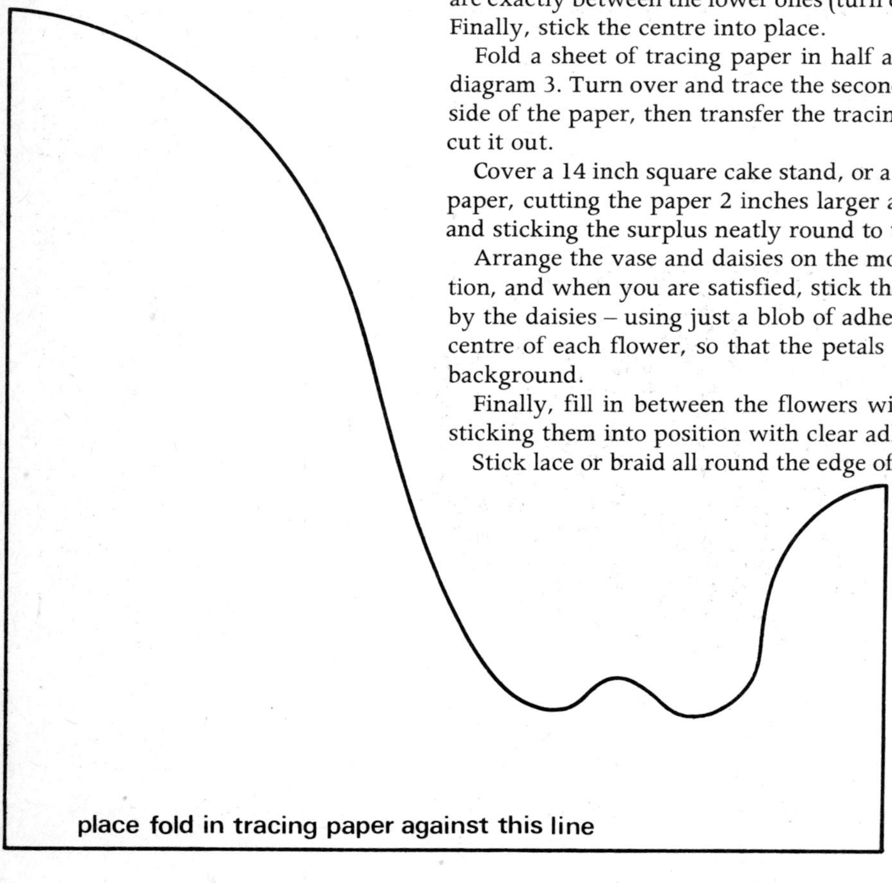

Cut another daisy shape in buff paper, and crease the petals in exactly the same way.

Trace the petal shape in diagram 2 on to thin card, and use as a pattern to cut eight petals in white crêpe (grain running as arrows): to do this, fold a strip of crêpe (*along* the grain) into eight, draw round the petal pattern on top of the folded paper, and then cut all eight petals together.

Stick each petal (using fabric adhesive) to the buff daisy shape with a line of adhesive between the centre and the X indicated on the pattern (diagram 1): position the petals exactly over each buff petal, with the tips matching exactly at the centre.

To make the middle of the flower, cut a $\frac{3}{4}$ inch diameter circle (as diagram 1) in brown cartridge paper. Then cut a 2 inch diameter circle in brown tissue paper. Paste the top surface of the brown paper, and the back of the tissue, thoroughly (with wallpaper paste). Then place the tissue over the paper and draw it towards the centre with the fingertips, gradually crumpling the tissue evenly over the surface of the paper, using a knitting needle or the point of a cocktail stick. Brush a little more paste over the surface of the crumpled tissue, and leave to dry out thoroughly.

To assemble the daisy, spread a blob of adhesive in the centre of the brown shape, then place the buff one on top, so that the upper petals are exactly between the lower ones (turn over to check this at the back). Finally, stick the centre into place.

Fold a sheet of tracing paper in half and trace the vase shape from diagram 3. Turn over and trace the second half of the vase on the other side of the paper, then transfer the tracing to your textured paper and cut it out.

Cover a 14 inch square cake stand, or a piece of stiff card, with black paper, cutting the paper 2 inches larger all round, mitring the corners and sticking the surplus neatly round to the back.

Arrange the vase and daisies on the mount, as shown in the illustration, and when you are satisfied, stick the vase into position, followed by the daisies – using just a blob of adhesive at the back to secure the centre of each flower, so that the petals stand slightly away from the background.

Finally, fill in between the flowers with short pieces of grasshead, sticking them into position with clear adhesive.

Stick lace or braid all round the edge of the mount, to frame.

8 Assemblage

This is a semi-abstract form of collage which many people enjoy. It permits the greatest degree of spontaneity and freedom of all, since the basic principle is that you gather together a varied selection of items – and mount them down in whatever arrangement you please. Almost the only "rule" is that in coming together, they form some kind of association, and are connected by some common subject in one way or another.

Assemblage offers such a wide variety of individual treatments that it is difficult to generalise. But it can take the form of a montage of photographs or other illustrations cut from magazines and newspapers, etcetera (as well as your own artwork), pieces of printed matter and so on – superimposed to create an intriguing picture. One cut-out can be stuck over another, and figures or other objects need not be in proportion: just so long as the relationship of the various "ingredients" appeals to you. Sometimes amusing, sometimes sad, montages usually convey some deeper meaning, or make a point.

A more symbolic form of assemblage is a collection of "found objects" interpreted in an artistic arrangement intended to depict a particular situation, emotion or relationship.

Originally unrelated personal possessions like travel tickets, luggage labels, foreign coins, a picture postcard, hotel menu, concert programme, etcetera, might be mounted down together in an assemblage entitled "Souvenirs" – mementoes of a holiday abroad. "Coming-of-age" could be composed of birthday cards and gift tags, a torn scrap of fancy wrapping paper, a decorative key, cake decorations and a champagne bottle label. Pins, paper clips and fasteners, an uneven piece of ink-stained blotting paper, a scribbled sheet torn from a spiral notebook and the worn cover of a dictionary (this could be cut from the wrap-around dust jacket) would symbolise "The Writer". As before, unrelated items are connected by a common theme. But the assembled pieces can be as three-dimensional and "real" as you like – only governed by convenience in mounting down. In fact, it isn't even necessary to stick the pieces on a mount: large objects like bicycles, furniture and pieces of machinery are fused together by some well-known artists to create abstract "sculptures". So have a look in the attic for inspiration if this kind of fancy takes you!

I have created two quite different assemblages – one because it amused me, the other with a feeling of nostalgia. Both emphasise the intensely personal aspect of this form of collage: but I hope the above brief explanation and my examples will give you the enthusiasm to inspire equally individual assemblages of your own.

Reading Matter

Illustrated in colour on page 61

A catalogue urging me to "Give a magazine subscription for Christmas" inspired this one. Each magazine was represented by a miniature illus-

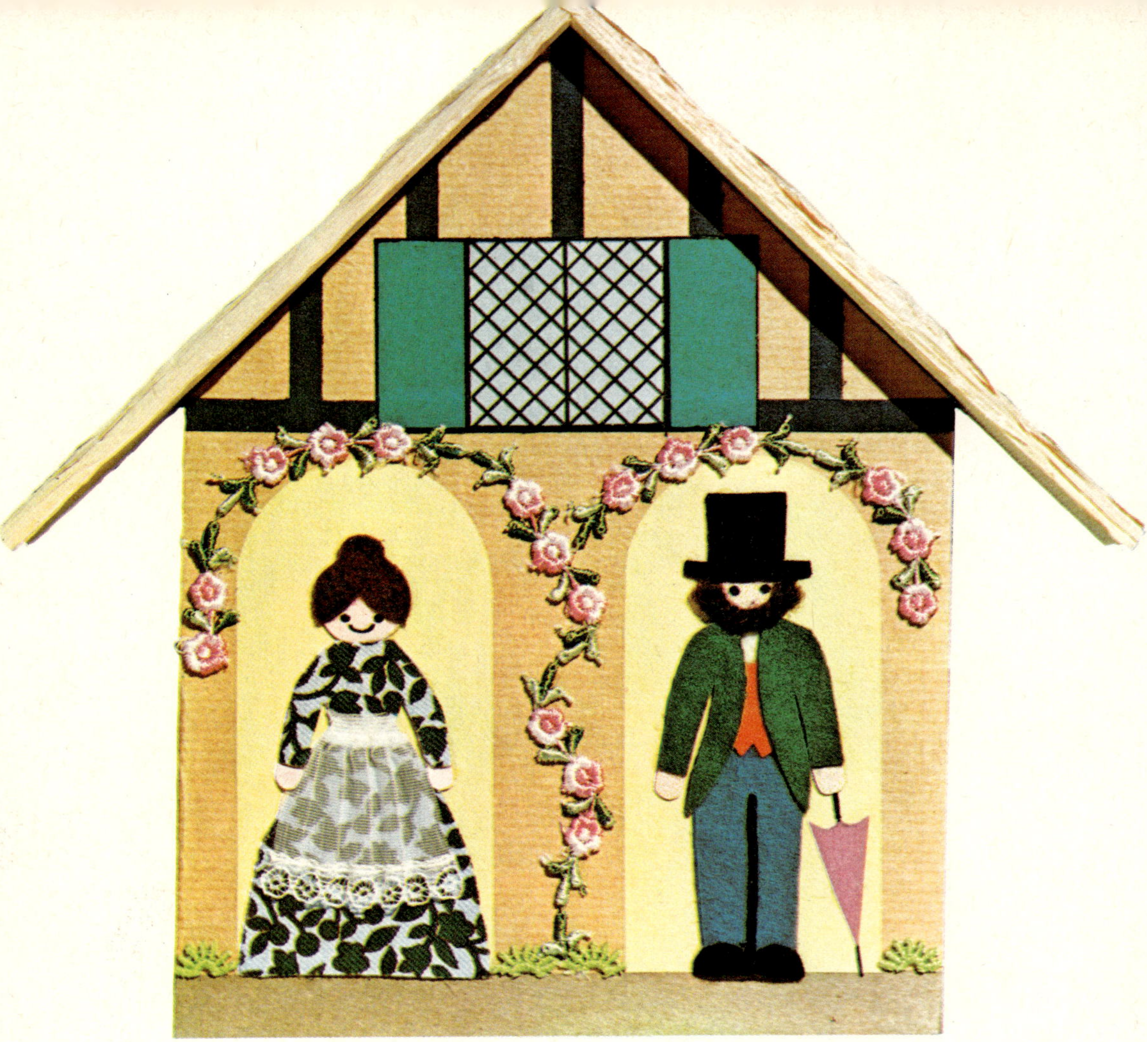

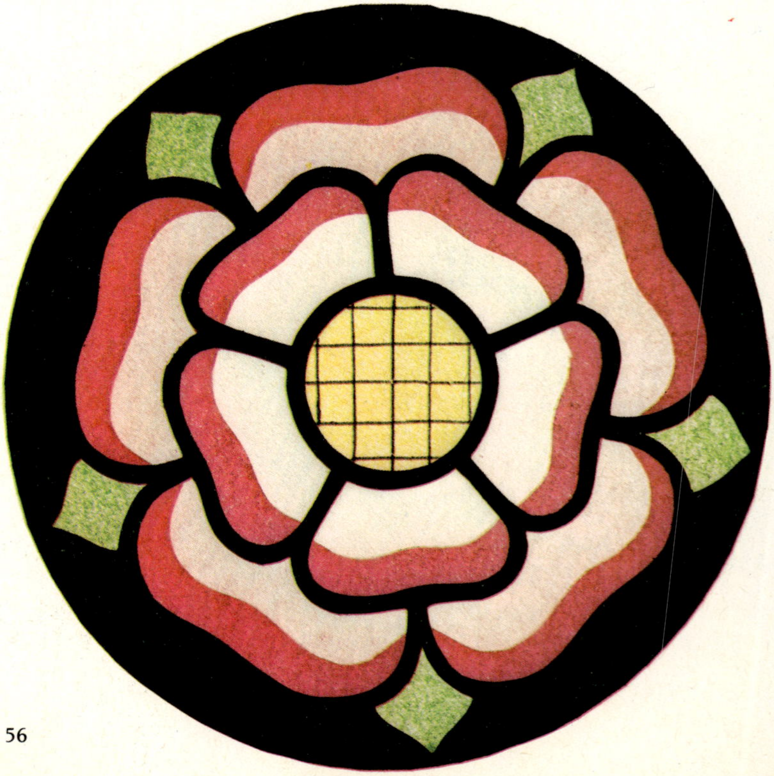

(Above) Weather House
(Right) 'Stained glass' Tudor Rose
(Opposite) Tudor Lady

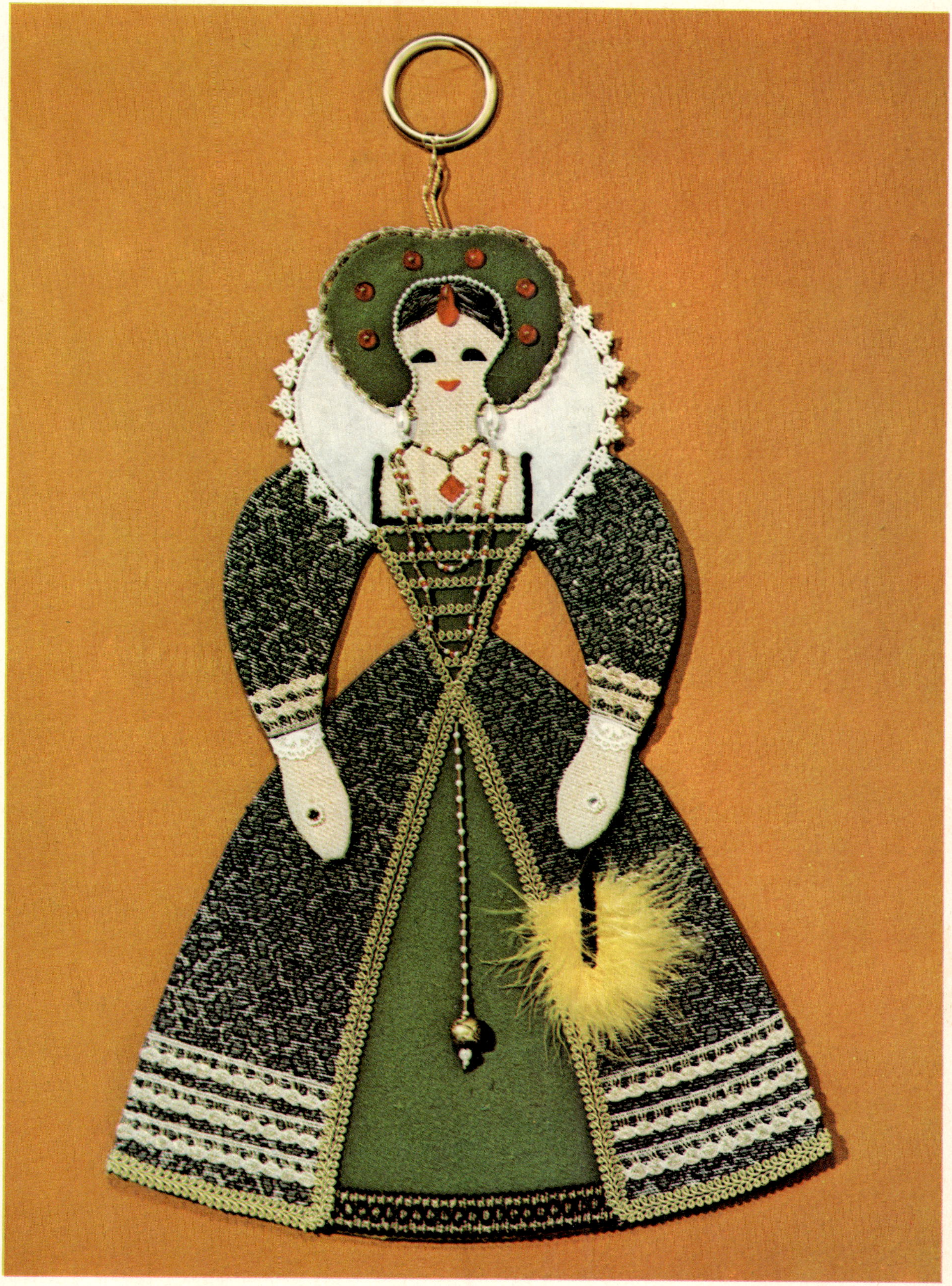

tration of the cover. These doll-sized reproductions so fascinated me that I thought they would make an intriguing and amusing montage.

I cut out the illustrations with a sharp knife, then pasted them down in two circles on a square mount – with, appropriately, a *Reader's Digest* in the centre – on a background of plain brown parcel wrapping paper.

Country Memories

Illustrated in colour on page 53

This evocative assemblage is essentially a composition of textures. Rough wood contrasts with fluffy feathers, hessian with smooth suede and tough leather, coarsely woven linen with fluffy lambswool, unbleached yarn with shaded wools, canvas and raffia with leaves, grasses and a dried flower head. And the colours are as subtle and near to nature as the countryside itself.

As an indication of the order in which I worked to create this particular collage, I began by collecting an example of anything which suggested the countryside to me personally. A scrap of hessian, a square of canvas, some dark green linen, a small off-cut of lambswool, straws of raffia, twists of shaded knitting wools and unbleached yarn, suede, leather and soft chamois cuttings, coloured feathers, leaves, grasses, honesty petals and a straw-daisy. All in a "country" colour-scheme of softly toning greens, yellows, browns and neutral shades bleached by the sun.

I prepared a 12 inch square mount, covering it with the matt side of the same brown parcel wrapping paper as I used for the previous collage, the outer edge bound with a simple braid woven from unbleached soft cotton.

Then I arranged all my components on the background, moving them around until I felt each looked "at home" in its surroundings and in relation to its neighbours, studying shape, form, texture and colouring. Keeping everything carefully in position, I mounted each item down separately (sometimes one over another – see the illustration), using the most appropriate adhesive – either clear all-purpose, do-it-yourself fabric, or double-sided tape (see examples of similar items in previous collages).

9 Unusual techniques

Here are two slightly off-beat forms of collage to fire your imagination. The subjects and treatments I have chosen are merely an indication of the scope which both methods offer.

The first method – working your design on a bed of Plasticine – is particularly suitable for bold, slightly amusing subjects, and abstract arrangements of found objects ranging from nuts, bolts and screws to pieces of dismantled machinery, making it an ideal medium for assemblages. The second method – creating a stained glass effect with coloured tissue papers – is as delicate as the first is robust. This lends itself especially well to designs with a religious theme: a strikingly simple Virgin and Child for Christmas – or a decoration of gay snowflakes in brightly contrasting colours.

These vastly different techniques have one thing in common. Both rely on light for maximum effect. The fish should be hung in a well-lit spot where the sparkling sequins will have a three-dimensional effect and catch the light to give the design movement, whilst the "stained glass" Tudor rose should be hung either in front of a window, or with a light behind it, to emphasise the glowing colours.

The Ocean Bed

Illustrated in colour on page 53

Underwater sparkle relies on sequins and pearls in deep-sea blues, greens, silver and mother-of-pearl. Let yourself go at the sequin counter, and then let your choice dictate the actual composition of your fish. Shiny raffia provides the essential seaweed . . . and those glistening shells on the sea-bed: remember Contrary Mary's garden in chapter 2?

Materials:

1 lb. pack lilac Plasticine
Narrow silver tinsel braid
Sequins in assorted sizes and shapes – in silver, green, blue and mother-of-pearl (see below)
Tiny seed pearls
Pearly button or bead for eye
Tiny coloured beads
Small shells
Shiny green raffia
10 inch square cake stand, or stiff card, hardboard or wood, 10 inches by 7 inches
Strip of thin wood 1 inch wide
1 yard braid to frame
Pins
Do-it-yourself fabric adhesive (optional)
Clear all-purpose adhesive

Method: Begin by cutting your cake stand or alternative backing to

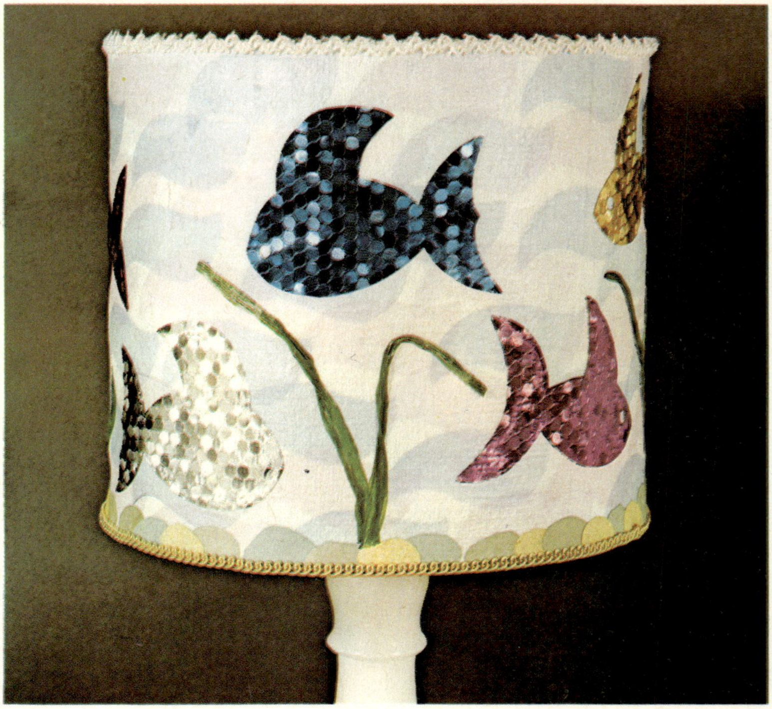

(Right) Aquarium Lampshade
(Below) Christmas and general occasion greetings cards.

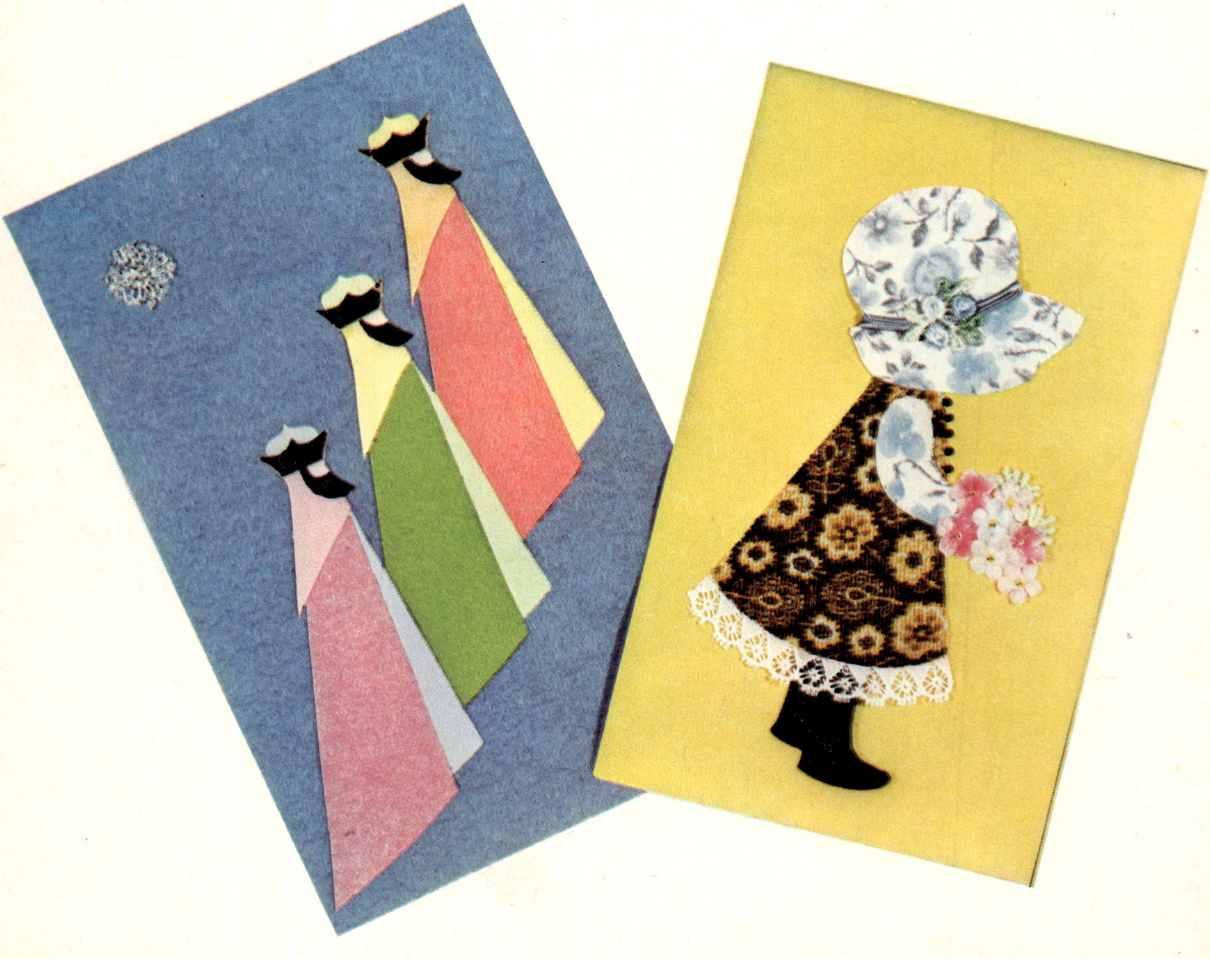

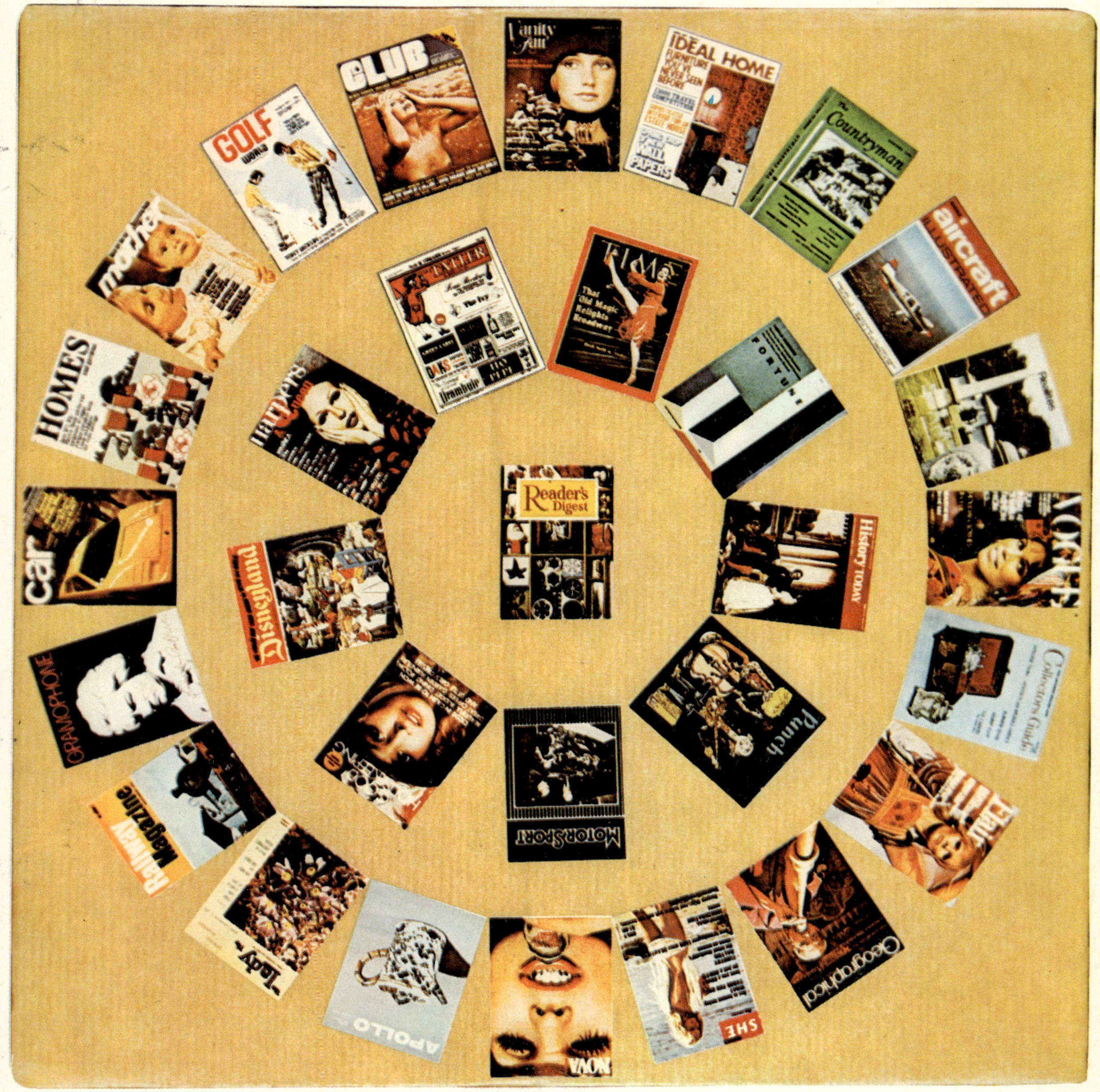

Reading Matter

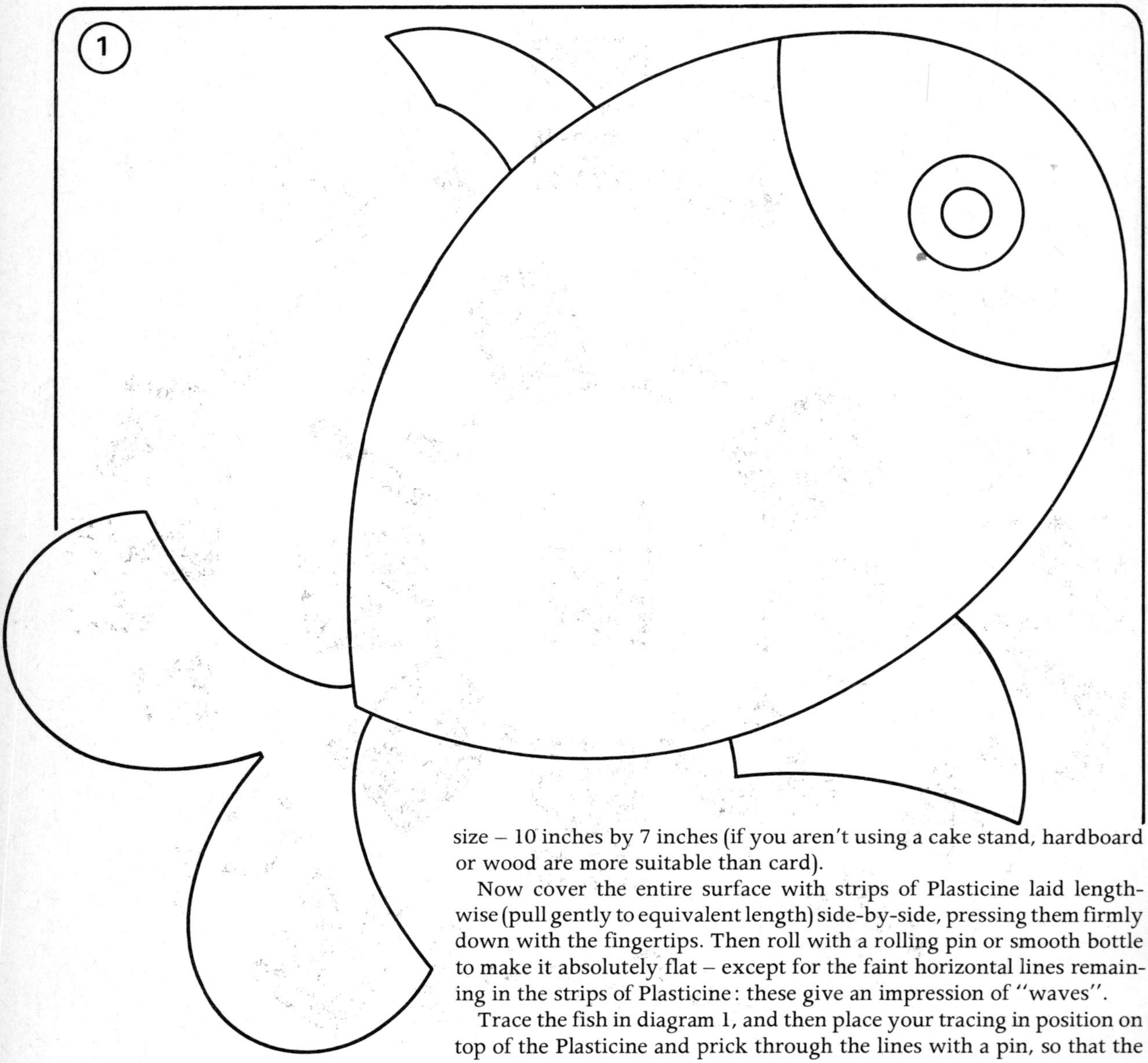

size – 10 inches by 7 inches (if you aren't using a cake stand, hardboard or wood are more suitable than card).

Now cover the entire surface with strips of Plasticine laid lengthwise (pull gently to equivalent length) side-by-side, pressing them firmly down with the fingertips. Then roll with a rolling pin or smooth bottle to make it absolutely flat – except for the faint horizontal lines remaining in the strips of Plasticine: these give an impression of "waves".

Trace the fish in diagram 1, and then place your tracing in position on top of the Plasticine and prick through the lines with a pin, so that the shape is transferred to the background.

Outline the body of the fish with tinsel braid, as illustrated, pressing it firmly down into the Plasticine with the point of a knitting needle, cocktail stick or similar object, beginning and ending at the tail. Outline the back of the head with a row of (I used blue domed) sequins, pushed into the Plasticine at an angle of about 45 degrees. Then press the button or bead for the eye into place, encircling it with tiny beads and/or seed pearls (I made a ring of each – see the picture). Then fill in the entire area of the head with small (I used steel-blue) sequins, pushed in at an angle, as before, radiating outwards from the eye. Fill in the body of the fish with rows of larger sequins (I used $\frac{1}{2}$ inch diameter, alternating lines of silver and green), pushed into the Plasticine at an angle, each row close behind the previous one. Begin immediately behind the head and end at the tail.

I used long mother-of-pearl curved sequins for the fins and tail, cutting them to graduate in length for the fins, and adding to the design with round and long-shaped seed pearls, as illustrated. Press each piece in firmly.

Cut various lengths of shiny green raffia and arrange at each side, as shown, pressing them into the Plasticine with a pin drawn down each side of the raffia. Press shells and tiny beads along the base to form the sea-bed. I filled in above the fish with a few flower-shaped silver sequins, to add to the air of fantasy.

When complete, "polish" the surface of the Plasticine with the fingertips until it is smooth and shiny, and all fingerprints have been removed.

To finish, cut four 1 inch wide strips of wood (I used balsa) to form a frame surrounding the base, overlapping above the surface of the Plasticine at least ¼ inch. Stick and pin into place, then stick braid round the top edge.

'Stained Glass' Tudor Rose

Illustrated in colour on page 56

There's something timeless and very lovely about the design of the Tudor rose, which explains why this historical emblem has survived the centuries. It is attractive in so many settings, and its simple lines make it an ideal subject to demonstrate this particular technique.

You need a sharp craft knife – and if it does slip and you make an unfortunate cut, just mend the paper invisibly at the back with a strip of adhesive tape (preferably the kind with a matt surface made specially for mending paper).

Materials: Black cartridge paper
Tissue paper in pink, deep rose, crimson, yellow and green
10 inch diameter lampshade ring
Black thread to hang
Do-it-yourself fabric adhesive
Clear all-purpose adhesive

Method: On the *back* of the black cartridge paper, draw a 10 inch diameter circle (the same size as your lampshade ring), carefully marking the centre. Draw another circle, 12 inches in diameter, 1 inch outside the first one, and cut out round this line.

Trace the radiating lines in diagram 1 and, exactly matching the centre of the lines to the centre of the black paper circle, mark the five lines *very accurately*. Extend these lines out to the edge of the paper, so that the circle is divided into five equal sections like slices of cake.

Trace the design in diagram 2, ignoring the broken lines. Then cut it out so that it exactly matches your "slices of cake".

Place the tracing on one section of the circle of paper, carefully matching the centre point and the straight lines at each side, and transfer the design. Repeat in each of the remaining four sections.

Using clear all-purpose adhesive, stick the lampshade ring over the marked line, so that an inch of paper overlaps all round. Cut this surplus into small tabs and stick neatly back round the edge of the ring, finishing on the wrong side.

With a sharp craft knife, cut out the circular centre of the rose, the five inner petals, the five outer petals, and the leaves – making sure that a narrow dividing strip of black paper remains between each, as illustrated.

1

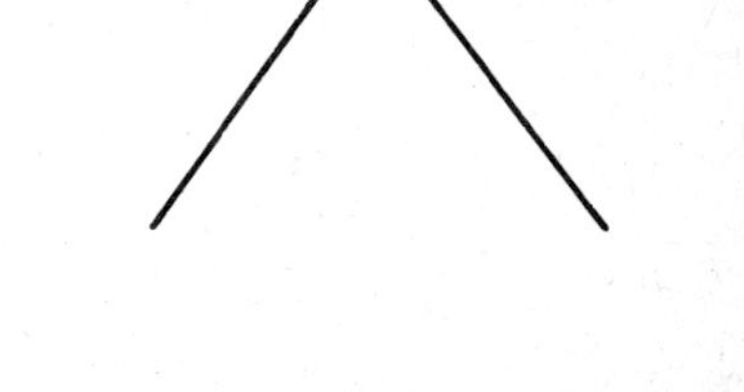

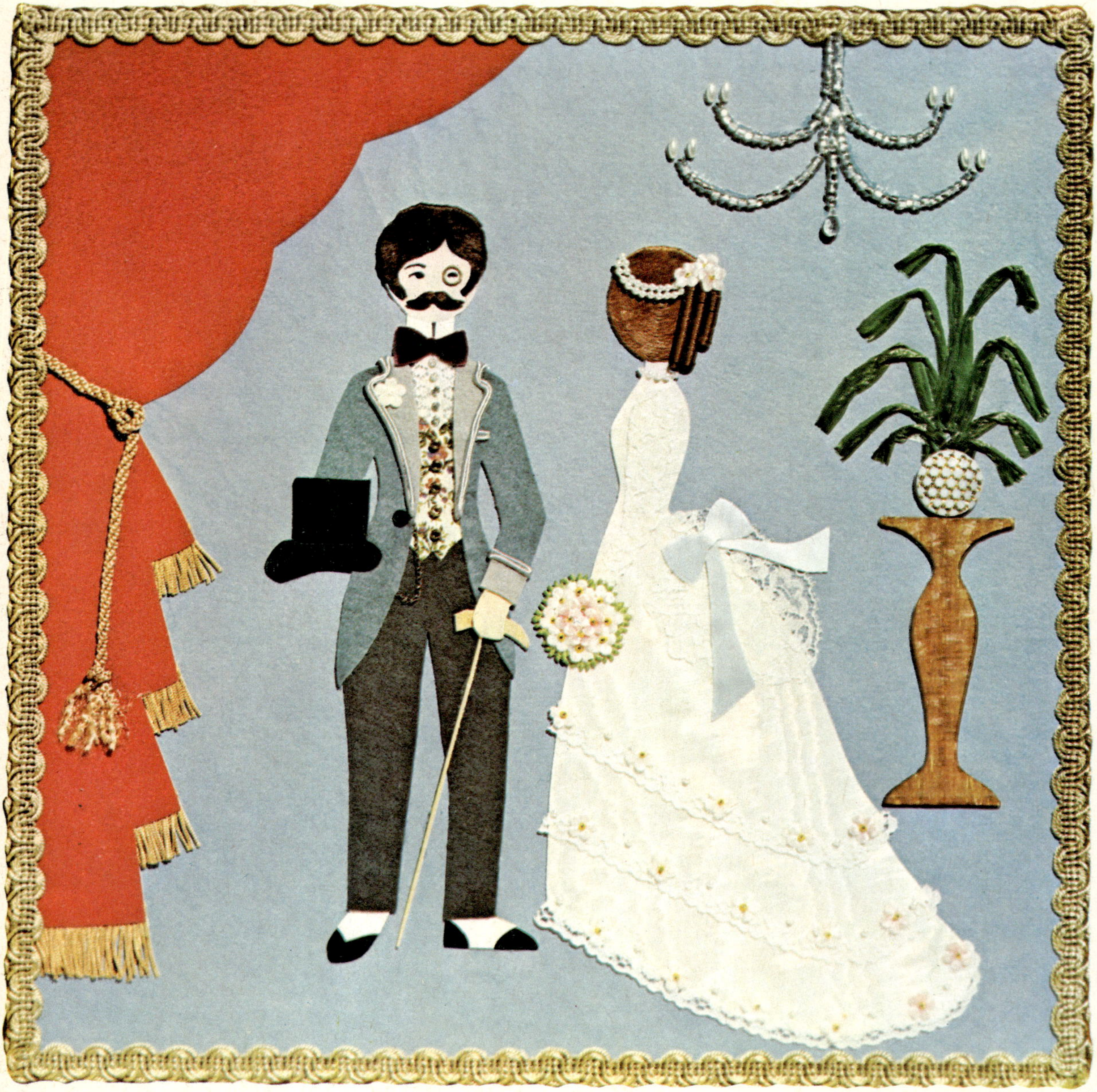

Love Story

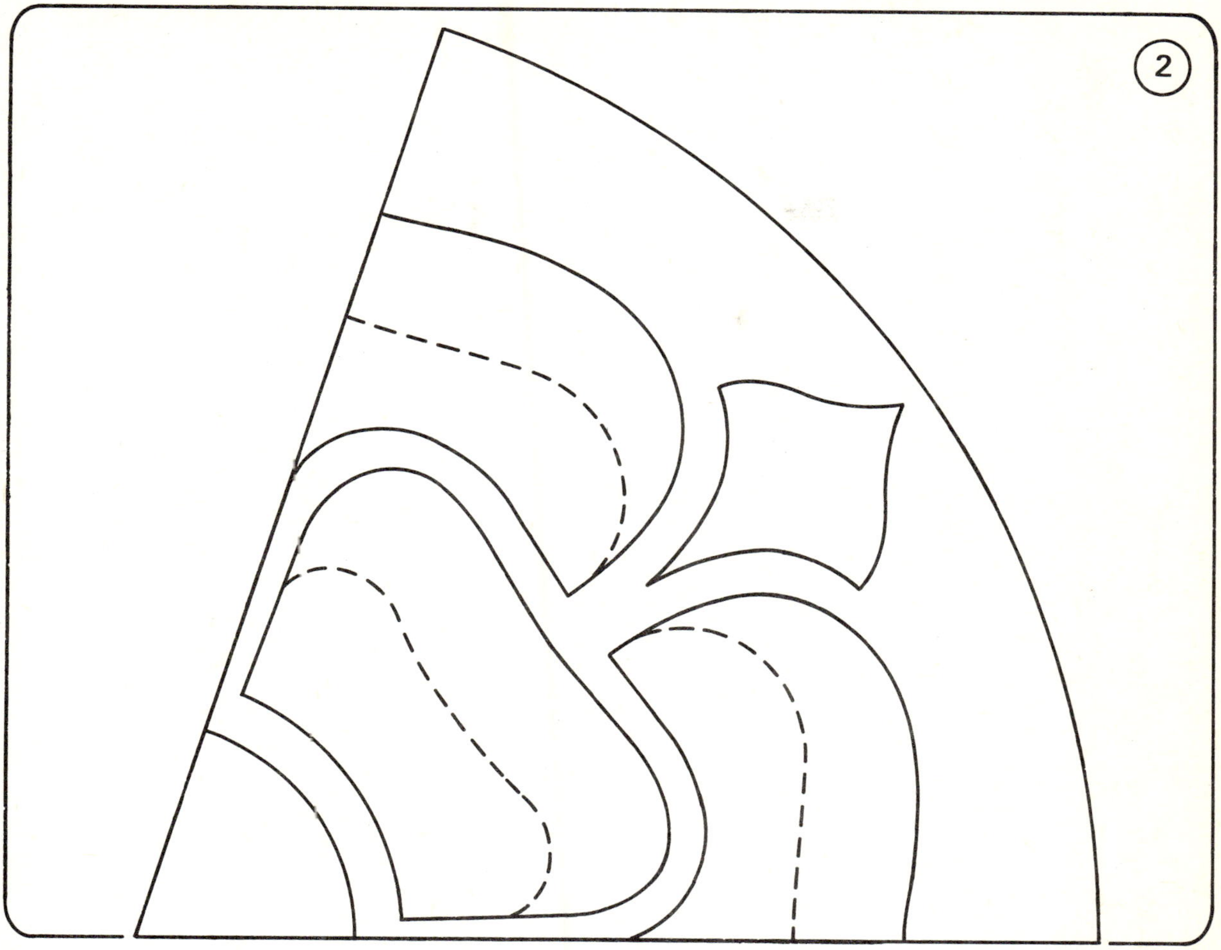

Now cut a circle of yellow tissue paper a little larger than the centre hole, so that it overlaps the black edge all round. Using fabric adhesive, stick smoothly into place on the back of the paper. Rule lines to divide it into $\frac{1}{2}$ inch squares with a black felt pen.

On pink tissue paper, trace the shape of the inner petal from diagram 2, overlapping the edge all the way round as for the yellow centre. Cut five and stick neatly into place as before.

On deep rose tissue paper, trace an outer petal in the same way (rule a faint line down the centre of your paper to match the side lines of the diagram accurately). Cut five and stick into place.

On crimson tissue paper trace the shape for the top of the inner petals, following the broken line for the inner edge, but overlapping the outer edge of the petal all the way round. Cut five and stick neatly into position, as indicated, behind the pink petals.

Repeat for the five outer petals.

Trace the leaf shape on to green tissue paper, overlapping the edge all round: cut five and stick into position.

Check repeatedly against the light as you work, and if you don't feel a shade is strong enough, cut another set of shapes in the same colour and stick behind the first ones, so that you have a double thickness of paper to intensify the colour.

Finally, fix a loop of black thread through the edge of the frame to hang.

10 Unmounted wallhangings

The technique of collage can be extended beyond the conventionally accepted "picture". Here are two vastly different examples of collage used to make free-hanging wall decorations.

The first is an amusing design based on the picturesque little "weather houses" which were popular years ago. The second is a rather more sophisticated interpretation of a figure in historical costume: for this one you will need to raid your jewellery box for old bits and pieces you no longer wear.

Weather House

Illustrated in colour on page 56

In these days of highly trained, expert meteorologists we no longer need such quaint old couples to forecast rain or shine . . . or do we? Unlike the old-fashioned variety, my husband and wife don't actually come in and out of their house according to the climatic conditions: I decided to strike a happy medium with each in their respective doorway.

One of my favourite cake stands makes the ideal base for this design: otherwise cut a thick piece of wood to shape. Whatever you use for the base, it must be at least $\frac{1}{2}$ inch thick. I have combined paper for the house with felt and fabric to dress the figures: but of course, you could carry out the entire design in paper.

Materials:

Brown parcel wrapping paper (or alternative – see below)
Coloured cartridge paper in flesh pink, yellow, green, blue, mauve, brown and black
Medium-weight Vilene or Pellon
Felt in grey, green, orange, brown and black
Patterned fabric for dress
Scrap of white lace for apron
Thick black embroidery cotton (or wool)
Thick brown wool
Embroidered lace flowers (optional)
Balsa wood (at least $\frac{1}{8}$ inch thick)
Natural raffia (or red cartridge paper)
8 inch square cake stand, or piece of thick (at least $\frac{1}{2}$ inch) wood 8 inches by 6 inches
Pins (optional)
Double-sided adhesive tape (optional)
Wallpaper paste
Do-it-yourself fabric adhesive
Clear all-purpose adhesive

Method: Carefully cut your cake stand or wood to the shape of the house in diagram 1.

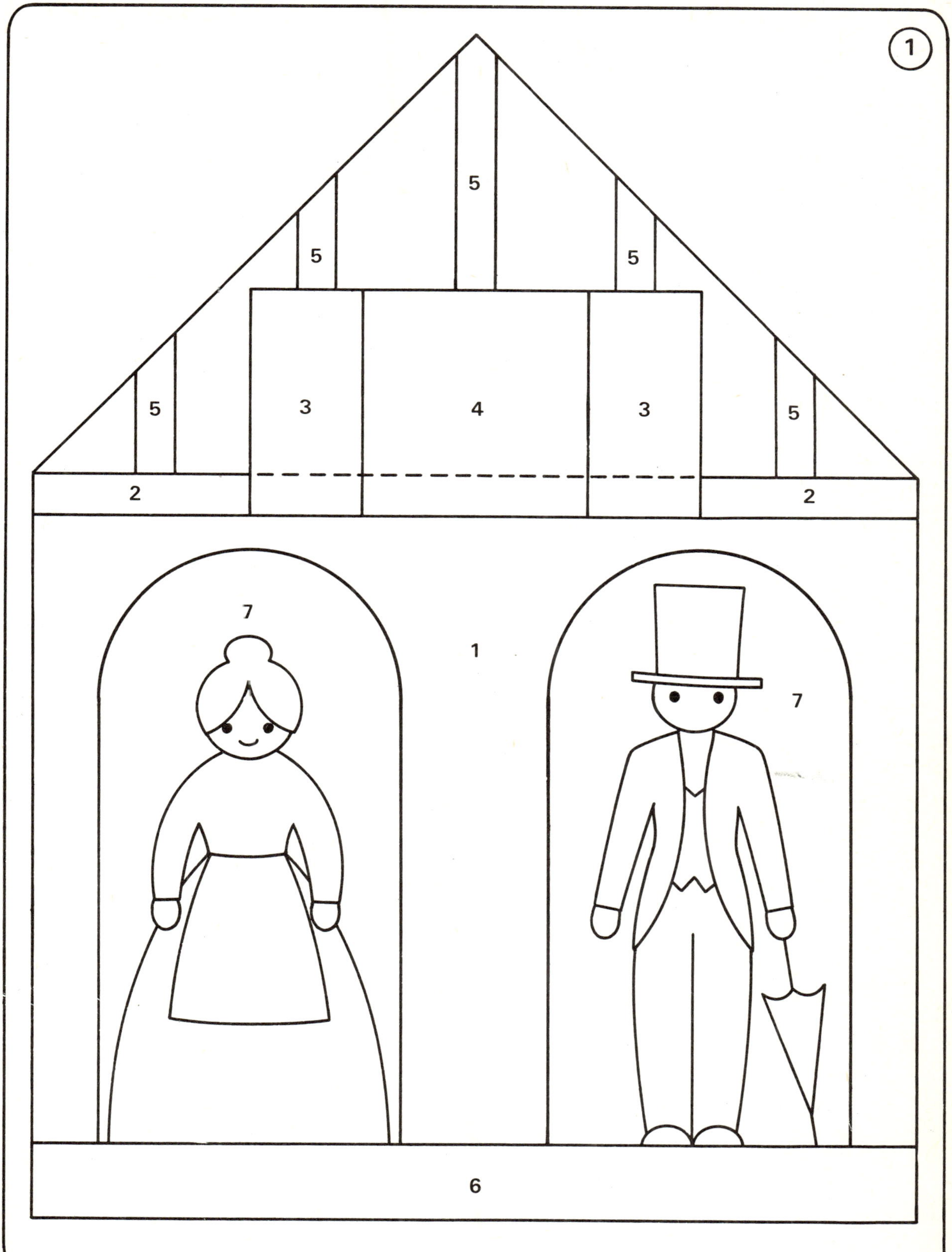
1
5
5
5
5
5
3
4
3
2
2
7
1
7
6

Paste parcel wrapping paper (or a similar neutral alternative paper) over the surface, cutting it 2 inches larger all the way round and then taking the surplus neatly round over the sides and finishing at the back.

Tracing from the diagram, cut the various shapes for the house in paper, and paste into position, working in the numerical order indicated. I used black for the beams, green for the shutters (cut in one long piece), mid-blue for the window, brown for the step and yellow for the doorways. Take the beams and step over the edges and stick to the sides as well.

Mark the four sides of the window every $\frac{1}{4}$ inch and rule lattice with a black felt pen, adding central division and finally outlining as illustrated.

Trace the two figures on to Vilene and cut out, then make up as previous examples, beginning with flesh-coloured paper for the face and hands, then the wife's hair in brown felt, her dress in fabric and her apron on top. Start with the husband's trousers in grey felt, adding a line of thick black cotton to divide the legs. Then his orange waistcoat, followed by the two sides of his green jacket. Cover the crown of his hat with black felt, adding a narrow black strip for the brim, with his shoes in black, too. Stick a scrap of brown wool round the lower half of his face for his beard.

Stick the completed figures into position in their respective doorways. Cut the husband's umbrella in mauve paper and stick into place. Then draw their features and complete the umbrella in black.

Stick embroidered lace flowers, or other decoration, to the front of the house, as illustrated.

Cut two 6 inch lengths of 1 inch wide balsa wood for the roof. Stick and pin into position, level at the back and overlapping the house at the front. Cover closely with lengths of raffia (I used double-sided tape to stick it securely), trimming the ends neatly: or cut squares of red paper and overlap all the way up each side of the roof to form "tiles".

Tudor Lady

Illustrated in colour on page 57

Once I have explained how I achieved my basic costume figure, I shall leave the decoration and jewellery to your own imagination and resources, only describing how I completed my figure as an example. So the decorative materials listed are only there as an indication.

As this spectacular figure is over eighteen inches high, the pattern is, of course, too large to be traced straight from the book. You will need to rule a sheet of paper into 1 inch squares (or use graph paper) and draw up your pattern from the diagram. However, as you can see, the basic design consists of only a few simple lines, so this is not difficult to do – and you can make it even easier for yourself by drawing only *half* the figure, at one side of the centre vertical line, and then tracing this on to folded tracing paper, the fold *exactly* level with the centre line: then turn the paper over and trace the other side of the figure from the first tracing before unfolding the paper.

It is essential to use a thick, heavy card to make a satisfactory hanging figure: but I used a thinner card for the hands.

Materials:
Thick, heavy card
Lighter-weight stiff card
Natural hessian (or alternative fabric or felt)
Brocade (or alternative) for gown
Velvet (or alternative) for headdress, bodice and kirtle

Materials: (cont.)

Medium-weight Vilene or Pellon (or stiff net) for collar
Assorted braids, coloured and gold, to decorate and outline, as illustrated
Guipure lace to edge collar and for cuffs
Tiny beads, gilt and coloured
Tiny seed pearls
Drop pearls
Large round decorative bead, and other odd beads
Diamanté and artificial "jewels"
Scrap of swansdown (or feathers) for fan
Brown raffia (or wool) for hair
Scraps of black and red felt for features
Curtain ring to hang (optional)
Adhesive tape
Wallpaper paste
Do-it-yourself fabric adhesive
Clear all-purpose adhesive

Method: Draw and then trace your pattern from diagram 1, as described above.

Transfer the outline to the heavy card, ignoring the hands and the broken line indicating the collar. Cut out with a sharp knife. Cut the hands in thinner card, adding about $\frac{3}{4}$ inch extra above the wrists.

Trace a pattern for the face and neck area, then cut in hessian $\frac{3}{4}$ inch larger all round, and paste into position: where the surplus overlaps the edge of the neck and shoulders, cut into small tabs and stick neatly round to the back. Cover the hands with hessian in the same way.

Cut about ten 4 inch lengths of brown raffia (or wool) for the hair. Tie loosely at the centre with another 4 inch length. Now mark the position of the front of her parting, and place the lower edge of the centrally tied raffia at this point, taking the two ends of the tie up and sticking with tape to hold securely (see diagram 2). Then take the raffia at each side smoothly down and tape the ends as indicated.

Trace a pattern for her headdress and cut in velvet, $\frac{1}{2}$ inch larger all round the *outer* edge only. Stick into position, cutting the overlapping surplus into tabs and sticking neatly to the back.

Trace the bodice and cut in velvet, level at top and bottom, but allowing $\frac{1}{2}$ inch extra down each side. Stick into position, finishing overlapping surplus fabric as before.

Trace the kirtle (underskirt) and cut in velvet, level at top point, but adding $\frac{1}{2}$ inch down each side and across the lower edge. Stick into place as before.

Trace the sleeve and cut twice in brocade (reversing the pattern for the second sleeve), allowing an extra $\frac{1}{2}$ inch all round except at the neck edge. Stick to figure, cutting surplus into tabs and sticking neatly to the back.

Repeat for the skirt, allowing extra at sides and lower edge, but cut the waist and edge of the front opening level. Stick carefully into position.

Now stick the hands neatly into position behind the wrist edge of the sleeves, reinforcing with tape. Stick lace over wrists, as illustrated.

Trace the collar on to Vilene (or net), following the broken line, and cutting it straight (level with neckline) along the lower edge. Mark the sides of the neckline of the dress too, and slit carefully up these as far as the shoulder. Stick or stitch lace all round the curved edge. (If you mark the position of the head against the collar, it isn't necessary to

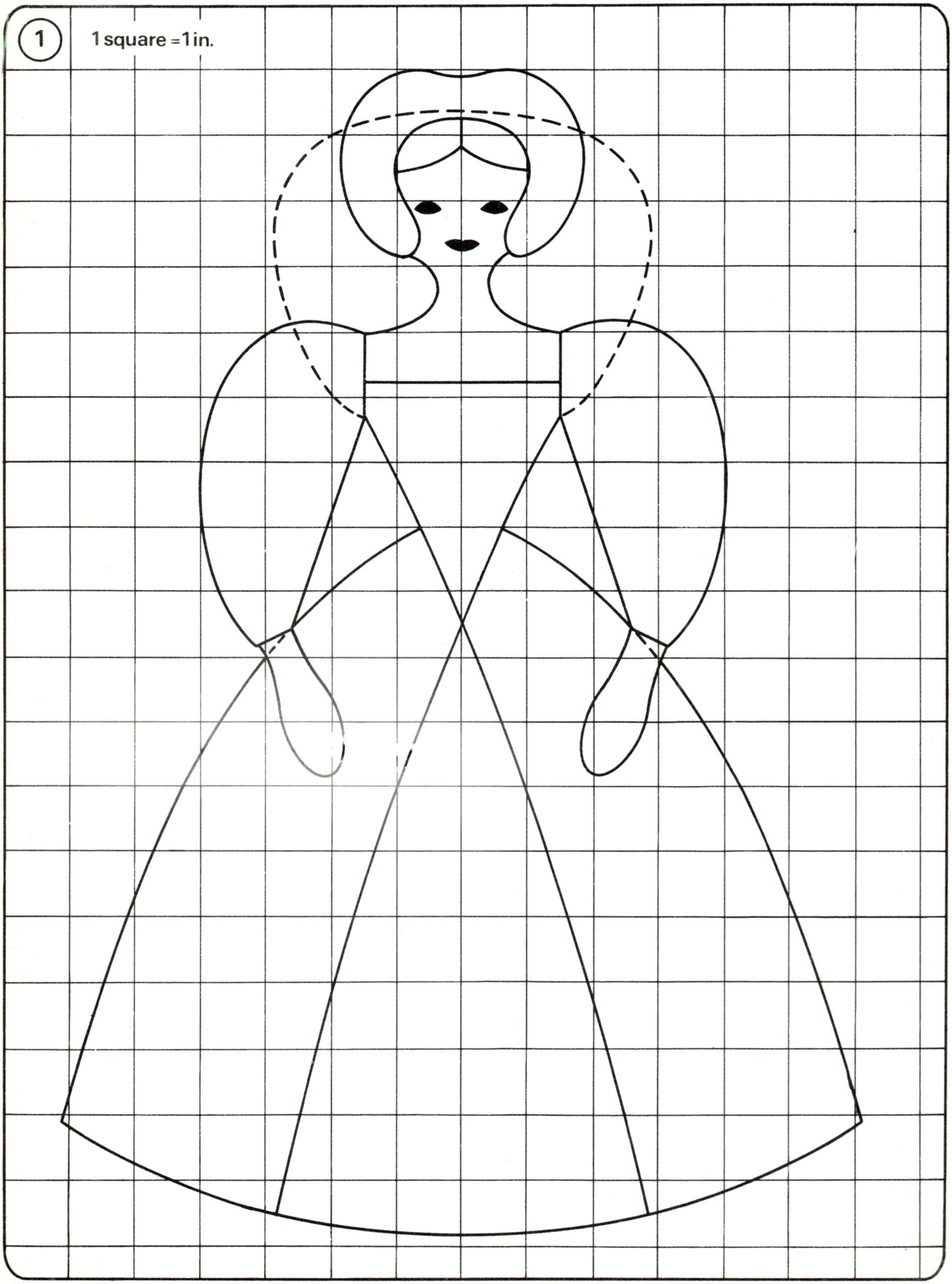
1
1 square = 1 in.

take the trimming all the way round.) I added a row of tiny seed pearls just inside the inner edge of my lace.

Decorate her headdress, following the illustration: I stuck a lacy gold braid round the outer edge, tiny seed pearls to outline the inner edge, and "rubies" (taken from a set of shaped plastic "gems" intended for children to play with) on the headdress itself, and at the centre over her forehead. I added a pair of drop pearls for her earrings, hanging them from cotton stitched to the edge of the card.

I decorated her cuffs and the lower edges of her skirt with bands of gilt braid (two and three rows respectively), taking the overlapping ends neatly round to the back. Narrow black and gold braid makes the lower edge of her neckline, and a wider design in black and gold decorates the lower edge of her kirtle. I cut silk braid in half to form the bands across her bodice and at each side, using the full width of the braid to edge her skirt.

Another plastic ruby forms the focal point of her elaborate necklace, surrounded by seed pearls with a crystal "teardrop" at the lowest point, and hung from a chain of gilt beads interspersed with pearls and red glass beads. Two longer strings of the same design hang beneath this: the ends of each are stitched neatly just behind the neck and shoulder, so that each row hangs in exactly the position required.

The "pomander" hanging from her waist is a large decorative bead, anchored by two pearls and suspended on a chain of gilt and pearls. Her rings are diamanté – red and clear – each surrounded by a circle of minute seed pearls.

Fix the collar in position as illustrated, sticking the two front corners to the front of the figure, and the centre behind her head and shoulders. I cut my black and gold braid in half to edge the sides of her neckline with black only.

I cut a 2 inch length of swansdown for her fan, sticking a narrow strip of card, covered with black tinsel braid, down the centre to form the handle – the top of which I taped behind her hand.

Trace the eye and mouth from diagram 3, then cut in black and red felt respectively and stick carefully into place.

Finally, fix a curtain ring at the top to hang.

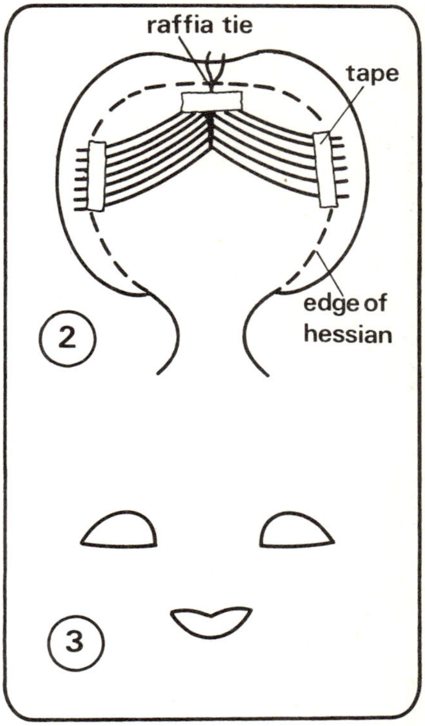

11 Practical applications

Far from being restricted to pictures purely for wall decoration, there are many practical ways in which collage can make life more attractive. Here are just three suggestions to set you thinking – all based on various techniques which we have explored together in the course of this book. These ideas are merely meant to stimulate your imagination as to the role collage can play in your own home.

Lampshades are specially exciting mediums for collage: here I have combined the tissue paper technique and sparkling fish theme of chapter 8 in a montage which changes completely, but is equally effective, whether the light is on or off. Plain place mats assume a very sophisticated air when tastefully decorated with your own individual falling-leaves design. And what could be more personal than hand-made greetings cards? You can make highly professional looking cards which will nevertheless give far more pleasure than any you might buy.

Aquarium Lampshade

Illustrated in colour on page 60

Lampshades and collage are made for each other. You're not merely decorating a plain background, but creating something which will undergo a subtle change to give a completely different effect when the lamp is lit. Of course, you must bear this in mind when planning your design – which is why I have made use of superimposed tissue, metallic and thick cartridge papers combined in a montage with waving strands of raffia "seaweed".

Although I have chosen an amusing subject, collage offers ample opportunity to create the most sophisticated effects, too. Dried, pressed leaves, for instance, or delicate grass seed heads, mounted on an absolutely plain ground. Or simply overlapping scraps of roughly torn tissue paper in either two or three shades of the same colour, or toning colours.

Materials:

- White lampshade parchment (or thin card) 30 inches by 8 inches
- Tissue papers in pale blue and pale mauve
- Metallic foil papers in deep blue, purple, silver and gold (or alternatives)
- Cartridge or other thick paper in dull colours (green, grey, sand)
- Green raffia
- Two 9 inch diameter lampshade rings, one with lamp fitting
- 1 yard white braid for top
- 1 yard sandy-yellow braid for base
- Wallpaper paste
- Do-it-yourself fabric adhesive
- Clear all-purpose adhesive

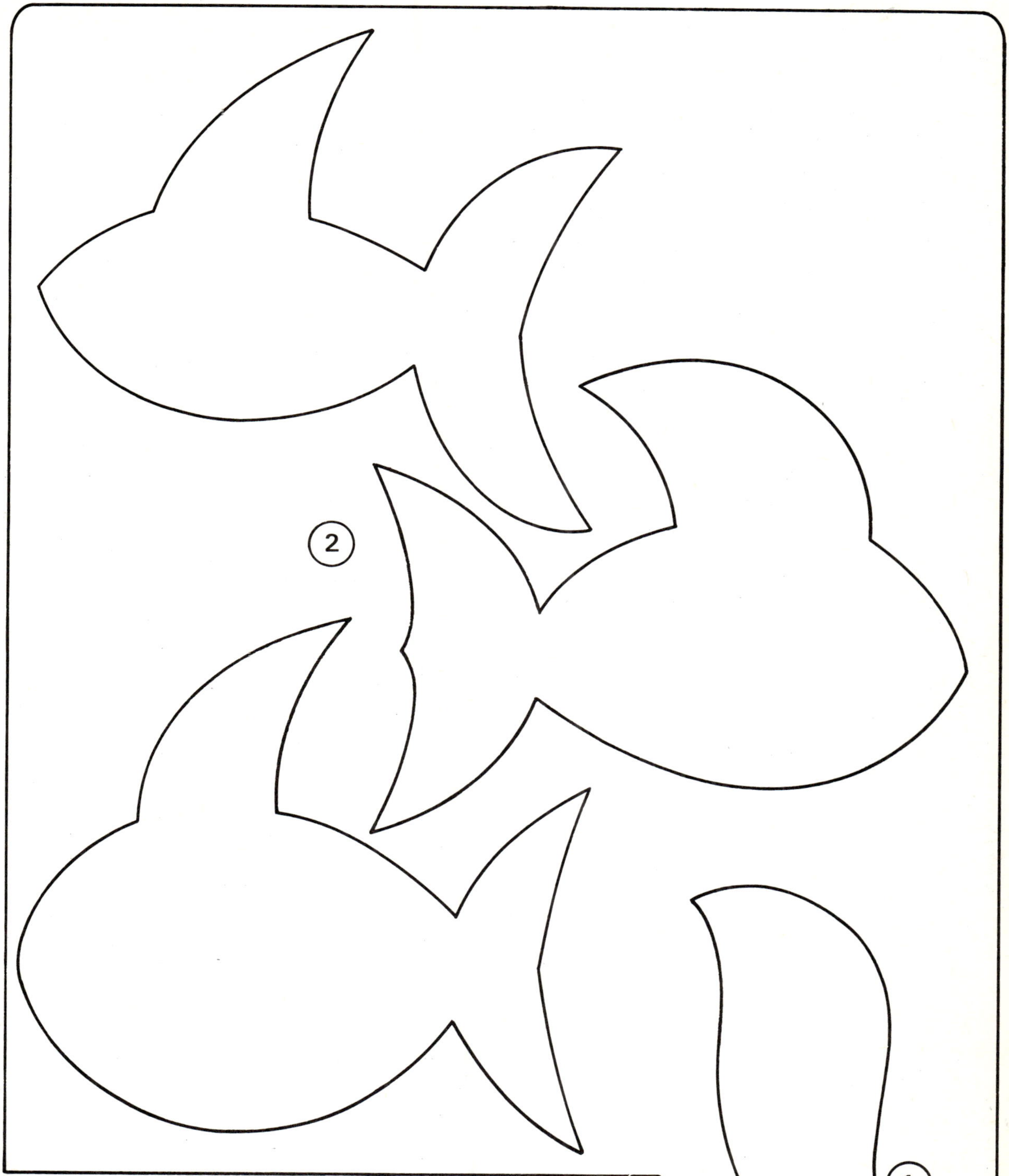

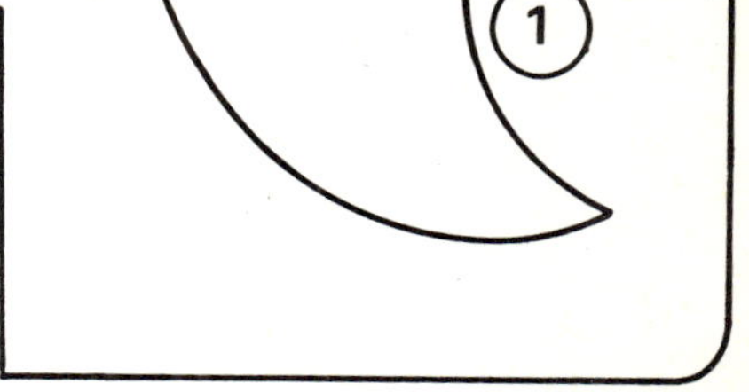

Method: Cut the lampshade parchment 8 inches deep and long enough to fit round your rings plus 1 inch overlap (about $29\frac{1}{2}$ inches).

Using double thread (draw it through a block of beeswax for added strength), oversew one long edge of the parchment all the way round a ring – but do not stitch the overlap. Then oversew the other edge round the second ring in the same way. Stick the overlapping parchment to make a neat join, then finish oversewing at top and bottom.

Trace the shape from diagram 1 and cut in card to use as a template to cut (from folded paper) a good number of "waves" in blue and mauve tissue. Paste these at random all over your lampshade, slightly overlapping as illustrated.

Design your own fish – or trace patterns from diagram 2. Cut about eight in various coloured foil papers. Punch a hole for the eye. I haven't marked these on the patterns because, by changing the position of the eye, you can alter the character of your fish completely. Using clear all-purpose adhesive (and making sure the surface of the pasted shade is quite dry), stick the fishes at different levels all round the shade.

Cut small oval "pebbles" free-hand in dull coloured papers, and paste them round the base of the shade, overlapping each other, as illustrated.

Cut short lengths of green raffia and saturate in paste, then stick at intervals round the shade, as illustrated, between the fishes.

Finally, using fabric adhesive, stick decorative white braid round the top edge of the shade, and sandy-yellow braid round the bottom, so that it slightly overlaps the "pebbles".

Christmas and general occasion greetings cards.

Illustrated in colour on page 60

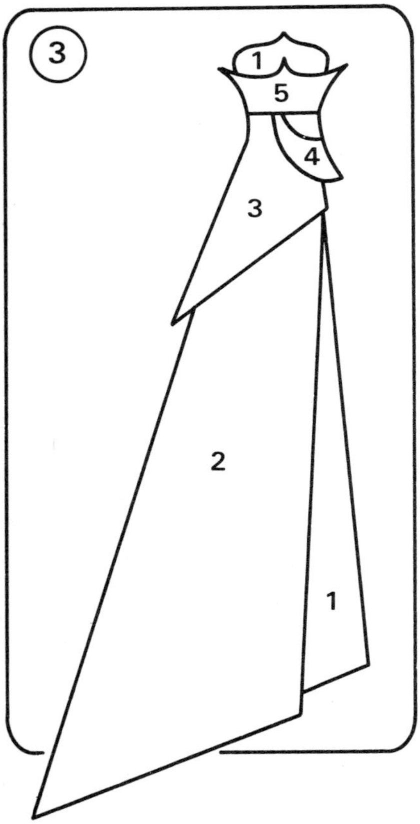

Christmas is an obvious time for your own collage cards, and the choice of suitable subjects wide: a thatched balsa wood stable, a straw-filled crib, a single dramatic star of diamanté, silver sequins and seed pearls, a jolly red felt and fluffy cotton wool bearded Santa Claus, a plump and perky robin made of real feathers . . . these are just a few suggestions. My own example is the Three Wise Men. In fact, it's only one wise man, as you can see from the pattern. But robed in different colours, the same design becomes the three kings illustrated on page

But nowadays nearly every occasion merits a greetings card, and collage is ideal for almost every one. A simple design using dried natural materials makes a particularly lovely card for a birthday or anniversary . . . or a simple subject like the one I have chosen here: a demurely bonnetted moppet presenting a congratulatory bunch of flowers.

Christmas card

Materials: Coloured papers in deep blue (for background), flesh pink, gold and assorted colours for robes
Silver lace or similar "star" motif
Paste or fabric adhesive

Method: Decide the three colours in which you plan to dress each king, choosing toning shades for each one. I chose lilac, purple and deep pink for the first, lime green, olive and gold for the second, and yellow, red and orange for the third – *using them in that order.*

For each king, trace the *whole* figure from diagram 3 on to the coloured paper you are using for the gown and top of his crown (see number 1 on diagram). Cut out.

Now trace the cloak (2 on the diagram) on to your second paper, slightly overlapping the headcloth (3), cut out and stick into position on the figure. Trace and cut the headcloth (3), overlapping the whole face, and stick to the figure.

Then trace and cut the *entire* face and beard (4) in flesh-coloured paper, mark the beard with a black felt pen, and stick into position.

Finally, trace and cut the crown (5) in gold paper, and stick that into place.

Cut a piece of deep blue paper 7 inches by 9 inches, and fold in half to measure 7 inches by $4\frac{1}{2}$ inches.

Stick the three figures into position on the front of the card, overlapping at mounting levels as illustrated. Add a silver star in the top corner.

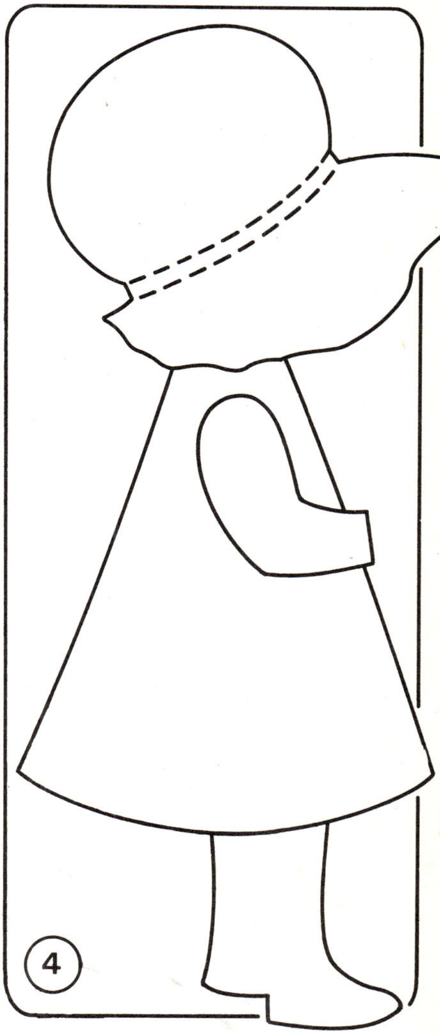

General greetings card

Materials:
- Coloured paper for background card
- Light-weight or medium-weight Vilene or Pellon
- Dark flowered fabric for the dress
- Light flowered fabric for bonnet and sleeve
- Black felt
- Narrow white lace
- Artificial flowers (I used forget-me-nots)
- Embroidered lace flowers (optional)
- Scrap of Russian braid or narrow ribbon
- Adhesive tape
- Do-it-yourself fabric adhesive

Method: Trace the figure in diagram 4 on to Vilene and cut out. Cut away the legs along the lower edge of the skirt.

Cover the legs and feet with black felt.

Trace a pattern for the dress and cut in dark fabric, overlapping the edge of the bonnet. Stick to the Vilene figure. Stick top edge of lace to back of Vilene, so that it overlaps the lower edge of the skirt.

Place figure over diagram 4 and mark position of legs, then fix them neatly back into place with adhesive tape.

Trace the arm only on to Vilene, then cover with light fabric and stick to the figure.

Cut the bonnet in the same fabric and stick into position. Stick a band of Russian braid or narrow ribbon round the crown, finishing the ends at the back. Trim with an embroidered flower or similar motif.

Cut a piece of background paper $6\frac{1}{2}$ inches by 8 inches, and fold in half to measure $6\frac{1}{2}$ inches by 4 inches.

Stick the figure to the front of the card, then stick flower heads to form a bouquet, as illustrated (I added a green guipure lace daisy, cut in half, for leaves).

Mark buttons down front of dress with a black felt pen.

'Ivy Trails' place mats

I've deliberately omitted any pattern for this design because this is one where you commune with nature to create an artistic collage! I picked ivy leaves from my own back garden – but you may prefer to go for a country walk or explore your local park for trees with interestingly shaped leaves . . . there's plenty of variety to choose from.

I bought plain vinyl covered table mats with a woven straw effect, then arranged my leaves on them to form a pleasing design (I show three alternative shapes as examples). Then, one by one, I removed a leaf and drew very carefully round it on to the back of some lime green velour-finish self-adhesive covering material. After that it was a simple matter of cutting the leaf shape out, peeling away the backing paper and pressing it neatly into position on the mat.

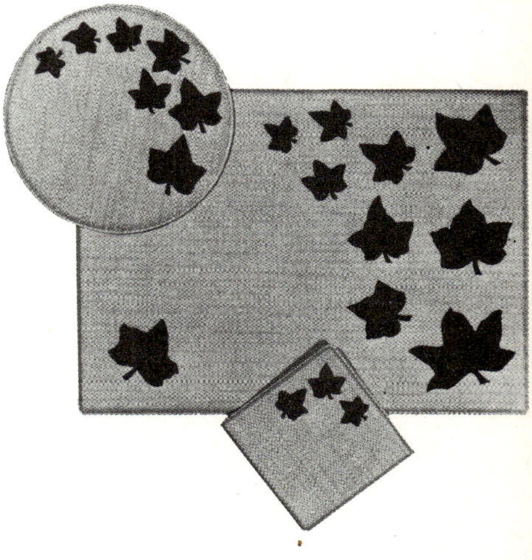

'Ivy trails' place mats

12 Grand finale

"Love Story" is the culmination of all the experience you have gained in the course of this book. Although at the beginning, it might have seemed too advanced or complicated for you ever to attempt, it should by now be nothing more than another exercise for your newfound creative talents. You will recognise techniques and treatments which we have covered together in previous chapters: this is merely a bringing together – a marriage – of as many of those methods as possible in a collage which is designed to display your skill to the greatest advantage.

I have not described each operation in detail, as you will already be familiar with the general methods of working, so I am only describing step-by-step anything which hasn't been dealt with previously – like patching a figure when overlapping occurs. Nor have I been specific about materials, just describing what I have used and done, since, having reached this stage, you will undoubtedly want to adapt and improve upon my original! Especially as you will want to make this collage, more than any of the preceding ones, your very own individual creation.

May this be the first of many. I hope I have been able to introduce you to the pleasures of an absorbing new interest, and sincerely wish you every success and much enjoyment in the future.

Love Story

Illustrated in colour on page 64

I began with the bridegroom, tracing the figure (diagram 1) on to medium-weight Vilene, and cutting it out as usual. Where the hat, at one side, and the hand and glove at the other, overlap the body, cut carefully round these so that they are free – and then "patch" the resulting holes in the figure with small pieces of Vilene, sticking the patch so that it overlaps the cut-away edge, and trimming it level with the line at the edge of the figure.

I pasted pink face tissue over his entire head, and when it was quite dry, made his hair from dark brown stranded embroidery cotton saturated in wallpaper paste. I began each side with his side-whiskers, following the hairline round and allowing $\frac{1}{2}$ inch to overlap the top edge of the head: I find a medium watercolour brush very useful for pushing the cotton smoothly into position. Having completed the side-whiskers, allow $\frac{1}{2}$ inch to overlap the side as well as the top of the head as you continue to fill in the hair area, pushing each new length of cotton close to the previous one. When both sides are completed, trim the overlap slightly and then fold it neatly over the edge of the head and stick to the Vilene, making sure no cotton overlaps the face area (as it may show through later). Allow to dry thoroughly.

2

Meanwhile, prepare his moustache by wrapping a short length of cotton round the tip of your finger, and then tie it tightly at the centre with a single strand of cotton (diagram 2). Trim the corners (as indicated by the arrows on the diagram), and then saturate the moustache in paste

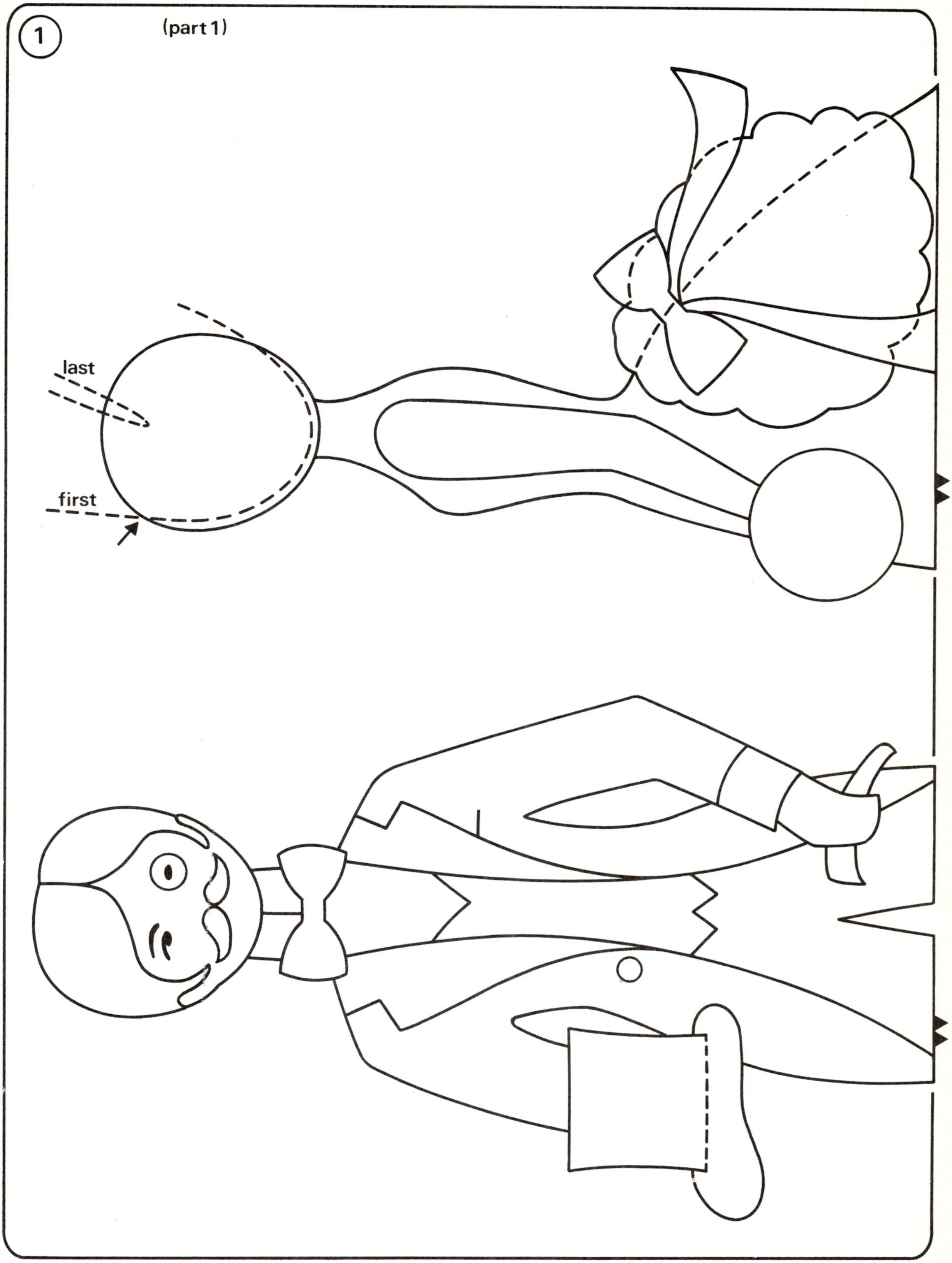
1
(part 1)
last
first

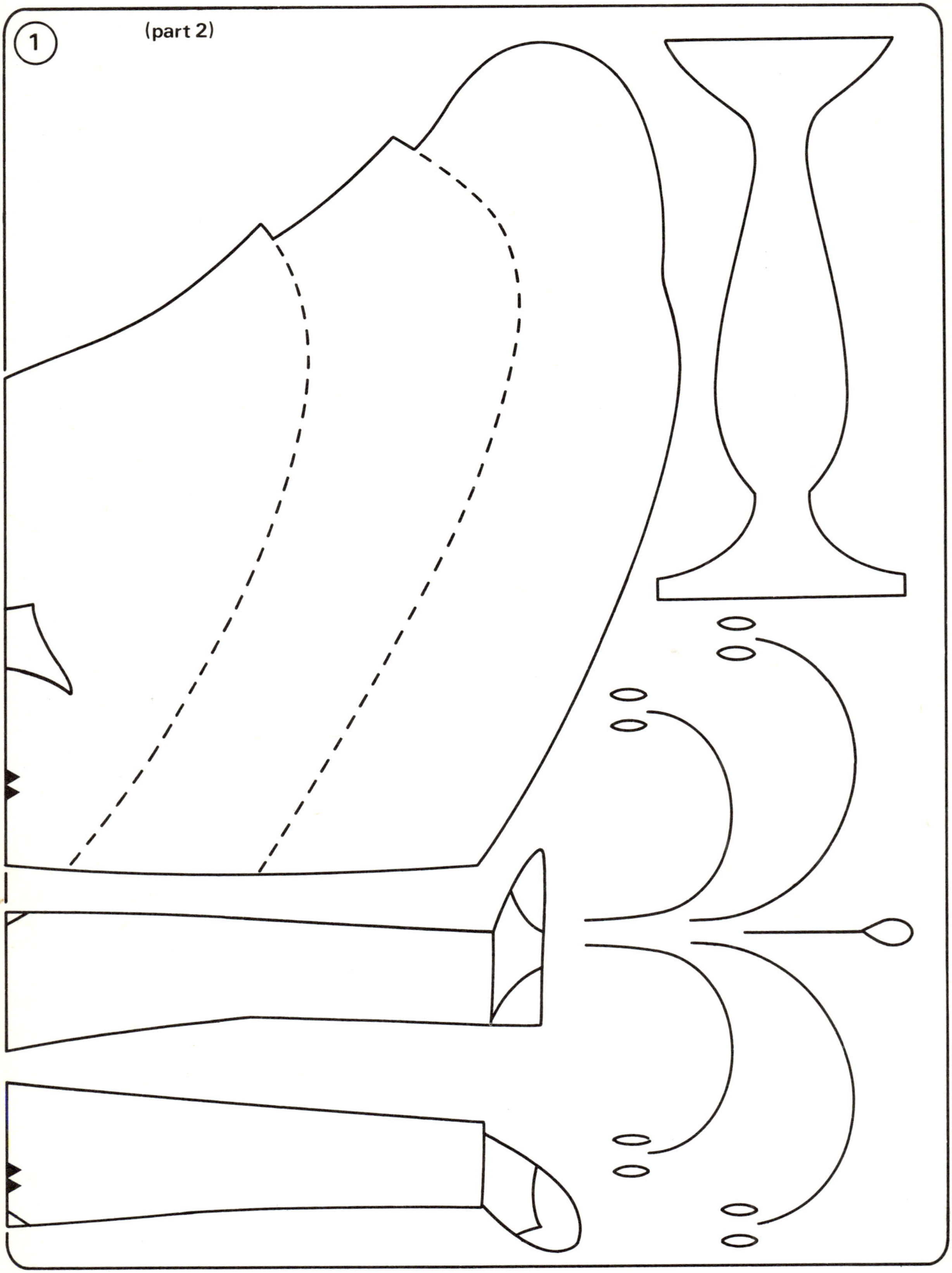
1
(part 2)

before shaping it carefully with the fingertips and both ends of your paintbrush, following diagram 1 and the illustration. When you are quite satisfied, place gently on a piece of kitchen foil and leave to dry.

I cut his shoes out of the shiny black background of an advertisement in a glossy magazine. His spats are white drawing paper – and so is his collar, with a black felt pen line drawn down the centre. His shirt is two rows of narrow white lace, the straight edges meeting down the centre, with minute "diamond buttons" prised out of their setting in an old brooch (these came later). I used chamois leather for his gloves, covering his hand and the one he is holding separately with different sides of the skin, to give a slight difference in colour.

His trousers are dark grey felt, followed by his waistcoat in a cream dress fabric printed with a tiny flowered design: small gilt beads made the buttons – at a later stage. I cut his jacket in mid-grey felt, *taking in the lapels,* but *omitting the cuff.* I stuck a tiny piece of silver-grey Russian braid across for the breast pocket, then cut the lapels and cuff in pale grey felt and stuck them into position, edging them with the same silver-grey Russian braid. His hat is black felt, with a band of black Russian braid, and his jacket button a circle of the same felt (using the largest size hole on my leather punch).

His bow tie is velvet ribbon, and as this tends to fray badly the moment it is cut, I traced the tie on to light-weight Vilene and cut it out. Then I spread fabric adhesive over the back of the ribbon, covering an area slightly larger than the tie, and pressed the Vilene shape down on to it. When the adhesive was quite dry, I cut the ribbon neatly, just outside the edge of the Vilene – with no fraying at all.

This is when I gave him his buttons and other finishing touches. His watch-chain (the ends stitched from behind) is part of a fine chain from a broken necklace, and his monocle one half of the clasp of a bracelet. His buttonhole is a single white forget-me-not head, and his cane (added after I had mounted the figure down), a narrow strip of bamboo from a cheap Chinese woven table mat.

I drew his features in with a black felt pen, and stuck his dapper moustache securely into position!

You will have noticed that, whenever possible, I prefer to leave women's faces to the imagination: I find this a wiser policy than trying to attempt a "portrait", which is usually less effective than the method I adopt. If you are a gifted artist, you will obviously find this no problem, but I have deliberately avoided the issue here although I have no difficulty visualising my bride's demure expression!

Having cut the bride in medium-weight Vilene, I covered her neck with pink face tissue and then did her hair in the same way as her groom's, using a slightly lighter brown embroidery cotton, and beginning at the point indicated by an arrow on the diagram, following the line round to the back of her head as shown – and ending with a short piece doubled in half in the centre of the U-shape formed by the first piece (also indicated on the diagram). Finish the overlapping ends at the back as before. To make each of her ringlets, saturate a length of embroidery cotton in wallpaper paste and then wrap it smoothly and evenly (but not too tightly) round a fine steel knitting needle about 35–40 times. Then slide gently off and leave on foil to dry.

I cut her dress in white moiré, backing it first with iron-on Vilene. Then I cut her arm in the same fabric and stuck lace over the top, trimming it level with the edge of the fabric all round. Having stuck this into position, I cut her bustle in the same lace, stuck that down, and then added the bow (in three separate pieces), which I cut from palest blue satin ribbon in exactly the same way as I had done the bow tie. I cut away the straight edge of some narrow lace so that it would curve more easily to decorate her skirt, then stuck three rows into place as shown, adding pale pink forget-me-nots, interspersed with seed pearls, at intervals along the top edge of each lace frill (the pearls are sewn from behind). A row of pearls edges her neck (these are stuck into position).

I cut a 1 inch diameter circle of Vilene for her bouquet, and stuck green guipure lace daisies all the way round overlapping the edge. Then I made a ring of pale pink forget-me-not heads just inside the green, filling in the centre with slightly deeper pink ones.

Now I cut the dry curls to length – two long (about $1\frac{1}{4}$ inches) and one shorter – and stuck them into position at the back of the head as illustrated.

I stuck two loops of seed pearls round the front of her head, as shown, with three deeper pink forget-me-nots topping her ringlets.

I covered a 14 inch-square cake stand with mid-blue paper, and laid the figures on it to plan their setting. I sketched a looped curtain at one side and cut it in rough paper which I used as a pattern to cut the pink velvet version once it was to my liking. I stuck silk lampshade fringe behind the lower edges, as illustrated, trimming it to length.

I cut the pedestal table (diagram 1) from thin balsa wood, sandpapered the edges, and coloured it with a pad of cotton wool soaked in brown ink.

At this point I mounted the two figures, the curtain and the table down on the background.

I added a sash of golden-yellow silk lacing cord to "tie-up" the curtain, making a loose knot above, and a tight one $\frac{1}{2}$ inch above the end – which I frayed out to form a tassel.

The ornate bowl standing on the table is a fancy button, and the aspidistra sprouting so healthily upwards, paste-soaked green raffia!

Finally, that splendid crystal chandelier is simply strings of clear glass beads, the loops held in place with clear adhesive, a crystal teardrop hanging in the centre, with candles of narrow, oval-shaped pearls.

I framed the scene with decorative silk lampshade braid.

Acknowledgements

I would like to thank the following for their kind assistance in the preparation of this book:

Copydex Limited: Copydex do-it-yourself fabric adhesive
Sellotape Products Limited: Evo-Stik clear all-purpose adhesive
Adhesive tapes
Harbutt's Limited: Plasticine modelling clay
W. H. Smith Limited: Stationery and artists' materials
F. W. Woolworth Limited: Household and general items
Arts and Crafts: 10 Byram Street, Huddersfield, Yorkshire.
General craft materials and equipment